Traveling the HEALING JOURNEY
Finding the Light in Mental Illness

Gina Capobianco

Gina takes you on an emotional journey through her mental health experience and it is a triumph. By guiding the reader through personal stories, inspired poems, and the real-life heroes in her life, Gina extends a message of hope to everyone. Her message will resonate especially for those who are experiencing mental illness, caretakers, and providers alike.

—Edward Portillo, Assistant Manager of Programs, NAMI Orange County

Gina's story helped me understand on a deeper, broader level the power depression can have over a person's life. I applaud Gina for her courage, her humility, her humanity in sharing her story, not for herself but for anyone who struggles with or knows someone living with mental illness. I can't recommend this book enough. Read it, share it. This book will change you; it did me.

—Tish Gamez, Simi Valley, CA

More by Gina Capobianco

Cognitive Introspection

Conscious Connection

Curative Quest: Mental Health, Hope, and Healing

A Light Amidst the Darkness: Illuminating Mental Illness and Suffering

Gina Capobianco is a mental health advocate, writer, speaker, and teacher. She lives in Southern California, where she enjoys walks on the beach and visiting her favorite independent bookstores. Find her on social media and on her website: www.ginacapobianco.com. She can be reached at ginacapobiancoauthor@gmail.com.

Social media

Instagram: @capobiancoauthor

Facebook: @GCapobiancoauthor

Twitter: @gina_capobianco

Traveling the Healing Journey: Finding the Light in Mental Illness
is dedicated to:

Dr. Richard Klein, PhD.

Dr. Catherine Sullivan, MD

and

Stephanie Debnath, PMHNP-BC

For their guidance and support on my journey.

ACKNOWLEDGMENTS

There are several people who have been instrumental in my personal journey and in completing this book. I would like to acknowledge them here. Their impact on my life cannot be captured in mere words, but I will try.

Dr. Richard Klein, PhD: Thank you for being my guiding light over the years. You have had a greater impact than you realize. I would not be where I am without you.

Dr. Catherine Sullivan, MD: Thank you for listening to me and for guiding me. You have brought me hope and strength. I would not be where I am without you.

Stephanie Debnath, PMHNP-BC: Thank you for guiding me through TMS treatment and helping me maintain hope. I appreciate you more than you know.

Carol Nichols: Thank you for being my friend and for being there for me.

Sarah: Thank you for being my friend and for helping me see things clearly.

Shannon Feldmann: Thank you for being my friend and understanding the journey.

Pam Martin: Thank you for always supporting and encouraging me. My coach, my mentor, my friend.

Carol Harrison: You may not be physically with us, but I still feel your presence in my life. Thank you. My coach, my mentor, my friend.

Cristina Rosales, PA-C: Thank you for understanding and recognizing that mental health is a part of total health. Thank you for treating me with care and understanding.

My family: Thank you for loving me despite my struggles.

Tish Pilelis-Gamez: Thank you for all our book talks and for supporting my writing.

Dr. Todd Hutton, MD FAPA: Thank you for making TMS available and providing me with the treatment.

Maria Perez: Thank you for helping me through difficult times at work.

Greta Vines Douglas, PA-C: Thank you for treating me with care and understanding.

Dr. Mort Rizvi, MD, FACS: Thank you for understanding that I needed empathy along with the surgery.

Lili Landaverde and Hector for providing extra care during my hyperbaric treatment.

Grace Slick: Thank you for helping me "Let It Go".

Zsuzsi Steiner of Zsuzsi Photography: Thank you for taking my author photograph.

Michelle Morgan: Thank you for editing Traveling the Healing Journey: Finding the Light in Mental Illness.

Michael Phillips: Thank you for your work on the layout and the front cover design for Traveling the Healing Journey: Finding the Light in Mental Illness.

Why This Book?

Why did I want to write this book? Originally, it was supposed to be a memoir, my story of living with mental illness. Early on, my writing took on a different shape, a different focus. My story begs to be told. Most of my nearly 50 years have been plagued by mental illness. There is a lot to share, but so many of the memories are missing, lost to the illness. As I wrote, it became obvious I was not really writing a memoir, at least not in the traditional sense.

This book is more like a conversation. One of my goals is to share my experiences, but I also want to explain mental illness. My story, like so many others, needs to be told. It is time to share my healing journey. This book is intended to advocate for more awareness about mental health. These are the desires that have created this book.

From the start, honesty has been my goal. I do not have all the answers. I am just a woman who has lived a life suffering from depression and anxiety. This book is my letter to others who suffer and my call to awareness to those who want to make a difference and see a change in the way mental illness is treated in society. It is my desire that you will find hope and light in this book despite its darkness. It is my sincere wish that the people who read these words will be encouraged to stand up and join the call to mental health advocacy. If we talk about mental health and make our voices heard, we can make a difference.

Some People You Will Meet

I want to introduce you to some key people in my story. They will be mentioned at various times throughout this book.

Dr. Richard Klein, PhD, my longtime psychologist/therapist
Dr. Catherine Sullivan, MD, my current psychiatrist
Stephanie Debnath, PMHNP-BC, the psychiatric nurse practitioner who oversees my TMS treatment
Cristina Rosales, PA-C, my current primary care provider
Shannon Feldmann, my friend, and the cover artist for my books
Pam Martin, my coach, mentor, and friend
Carol Harrison, my coach, mentor, and friend, who passed away in 2018
Carol Nichols and Sarah, my friends
Dr. Todd M. Hutton, MD FAPA, director of SoCal TMS

Other people will pop up in my story, but an exhaustive list is not necessary here. For some people, I will use their names. Others will be referred to by a made-up initial to conceal their identities. In these cases, I either do not have their permission to use their names or I did not want to expose them because of their actions.

1

Introduction

An Invisible Illness

I see it in the eyes of others.
They wonder how I can have an illness
When I seem to function so well.
My illness is invisible at times,
But it is always there.
Plaguing my mind;
Hindering my life.
I hold so much of the pain inside;
Pretend the physical symptoms are not real.
Mental illness is often silent on the outside.
Others do not understand what I go through each day.
They assume I am okay.
Sometimes I even tell them that I am.
It is my attempt to normalize how I really feel,
But it is a lie.
Mental illness hurts.
Invisible at first glance.
Devasting when truly seen.
If others could see the torment
Maybe they would understand and
Life might be a little easier for me.
The pain of an invisible illness is hard to explain.
So, I do my best to hide it.
When really I should explain it to anyone who will listen.
Let others know what it is like.
Raise awareness
And allow myself a chance to heal.

Depression is a thief. It has stolen so much from me over the years. As I attempt to tell my story, I question whether I have enough memories to give my story the justice it deserves. There are many facts and details, especially from the earlier years, that I do not remember. What I do remember are the feelings, the emotions that coursed through me. Some periods of my mental illness are clearer than others. I am going to attempt to retell my story. It is a story worth telling. Just maybe it will help someone else.

It is difficult to pinpoint the exact moment that depression reared its ugly head. It was sometime in the year 1988, the year I turned 15. George Bush was elected President. In all honesty, I had to search the internet to remind myself of what was going on that year. Evidently, George Bush winning the Presidency was the news story of the year. That election escapes my memory. Other things that happened that year include Rain Man and Who Framed Roger Rabbit were hits at the box office; a movie ticket cost $4; Roseanne Barr was arguably the most famous person in the United States; Johnny Depp, Tom Cruise, and Richard Gere were Hollywood's leading men; Lloyd Bentsen told Dan Quayle, "Senator, you are no Jack Kennedy"; the Dodgers won the World Series, and Nike's "Just Do It" ads were popular (https://popculturemadness.com).

What else was going on in 1988? The music was good. Of course, it was. It was the 80s. Although, my musical preference was the music of the late 1960s at the time. Jefferson Airplane was my favorite. One of their lead singers, Grace Slick, will enter my story in an important way later. My choice in music led my parents to believe I was smoking pot as a teenager. I was not, but I guess an introverted teenager listening to hippie music led to one assumption.

Even today I am rather introverted, though I have learned to be more outgoing when necessary. As a teenager I blended into the crowd. It was easy for me to go unnoticed, and I preferred it that way. Sure, I had friends, but it was a small group. Today I can remember some names, but I do not remember much of the interactions. That is a combination of the passage of time and the thievery of mental illness.

I attended a private high school, known for its academics and even more so for its football team. In the beginning I was a good student. Advanced and honors classes filled my schedule. Even as a ninth grader I was aware that I was accepted at that high school not as much for my grades, but so they could ensure my younger brother would play football there in a couple years. It did not really bother me. It was what it was.

My guess is that my initial high school experiences were similar to my classmates. Honestly, I do not remember much. I am sure I went to classes and attended the football games on Friday nights. Everybody did.

The depression appeared without fanfare. I do not remember the specific moment when it first hit me. I just remember it being there. A heavy darkness floating over me; shrouding me. I did not have the words to explain it in those early days. It would be several years before I was diagnosed with depression. In the late 1980s, mental health was not really addressed in families or schools. My depression went mostly unnoticed. I cannot fault anyone. Awareness of mental health did not exist at that time. That does not excuse the fact that I was left to deal with depression on my own. It is just the way things were. I do not harbor any ill thoughts toward the people who should have stepped in at the time. I am sure they thought they were doing their jobs the way they were supposed to do them. Sometimes people with mental illness just slip through the cracks and do not get the help they so desperately need. The high school counselor could have done more, probably should have, but I hold no bad feelings. My parents could have done more, but they did not know what was going on. I do not fault them. It is just the hand that I was dealt.

My journey with mental illness had begun. It is a journey I am still on today as I approach my 50th birthday. In the following pages I will share my story, allowing you to take part in my journey. I hope you gain something from the ride.

2

Depression Emerges – The Early Years

Child of My Past

Deep inside of me resides the child of my past.
A faceless soul who continually emerges,
Reminding me she is there even when I do not recognize her.
She has something to say,
But I cannot hear her.
Mumbled words expressed through pains I do not understand.
I fear this little girl.
Yet I long to know what she is trying to tell me.
Wonder if she has the answers.
Deep within me, she hides.
Forced into the recesses of my mind,
She battles with me,
Trying to escape;
Bring her secret to the forefront and
Release me from its pain.

It is the late 1980s, maybe early 1990s at a Catholic high school in South-ern California. I sit leaning up against a brown wall. The cool cement un-derneath me is hard, but I am comfortable here. This is my spot. I am alone. Other students walk by but do not notice me. It is just me and my red, spiral notebooks. The notebooks are my lifeline, where I write everything that is going through my head. These are not pleasant thoughts. My writing takes the form of poetry. There is darkness, a heavy weight smothering me. Thoughts of death fill the pages. As I sit against the wall the words spill onto the page. I do not know how to stop them. I do not want to stop them.

A bell rings, disturbing my writing. With hesitation I get up from my spot and head to a classroom. It does not matter which class it is. The classes are all the same to me, meaningless. How I manage to pass classes, I have no idea. I am just going through the motions. Just as at my spot against the

6

wall, I go unnoticed in the classroom. I am just a dark blob of nothingness.

It is difficult to look back on this period in my life. There are so many details that I do not remember. I remember being in pain, not physical pain, but a deep pain, nonetheless. I remember not wanting to live. Death seemed like the answer. I wrote poetry about dying constantly. Let the thoughts fill the pages of my red spiral journals.

As difficult as those days were, I need to look back upon them. So recently, I hung out with Sharon Raaen, a friend I have known most of my life. We went to school together from the second grade through twelfth grade. We lost touch for a long time after high school, but reconnected years later thanks to social media.

On this evening, I am at her house going through her old high school yearbooks. Mine have been damaged and discarded. The hope is to rekindle some of my memories. Maybe the yearbooks will trigger memories of what was going on at that time in my life; remind me that there was more than just the dark pain that surrounded me as a teenager. Sharon remembers so much more than I do. As we look at the pictures, she tells me about the different people we went to school with. Not only does she remember them, but she has kept in touch with many. I only have contact with a few on Facebook. If they had not found me on social media, I probably would not be in contact with anyone.

A picture of one guy reminds me that I was not alone in my darkness. As I look at his picture, I remembered the two of us waiting for our turn to see the counselor; both surrounded by our own darkness. In another picture I see a girl I had confided in on a few occasions. A memory returns of her telling the school counselor that I was talking about killing myself. She had the right intention, but it did not lead to me getting any real help.

The school counselor was kind, but I do not remember her ever doing much to address my depression. Seeing her picture brings back vague memories of her frequently saying, "one day things will get better." Even as a teenager, I knew those words were baseless—well-intentioned, but useless in the midst of depression.

The platitudes were present. The positive talk was meaningless because it had no meaning attached to it. People tried to cheer me up, students, counselors, teachers, but it never worked. You cannot cure depression with positive talk. Positive talk is just that, talk. It was useless to me. The "life will get better speech" meant nothing to me. I believed it was a lie. Just something well-intending adults said to deal with depressed teenagers.

Poetry became an escape for me. I am not sure how I started writing poems, but it became a huge part of me. The first notebook I wrote in was a half-page-sized red spiral notebook. Every notebook after that was the same. I am not sure why. Maybe it gave me a sense of security. Each of my notebooks had to be red, and they were all the same size.

Everything became about the poetry. I wrote constantly. My poems expressed the darkness I was experiencing. The poems were filled with thoughts of dying. Poetry was my outlet. I could write what I could not say out loud. Somehow, I knew I had to hide the darkest of these poems. The red spiral notebooks were never out of my sight. I carried them with me everywhere. One notebook eventually became six or seven. They were always with me.

As a freshman I had an elderly nun for English class. Something happened to her. Maybe she fell or became sick. I do not remember. A long-term substitute, Lesley Dahl, was brought in to teach us. She would be the one to encourage me to write. Again, there is a lot I do not remember. I wrote with a pencil in my notebooks. I was very serious about my poetry. Despite this, I did not understand how it was actually helping me. Now I know it was giving me a release for all of the emotions and feelings that the depression was creating in my mind. It was the therapist I did not have at the time, and it started a lifetime of writing.

When I wrote poetry, I never capitalized the word "I". Looking back on it, I was expressing what I felt was my personal worth. I believed I had no worth. I did not deserve the attention of a capital letter. The lowercase "i" showed how little I thought of myself. Even today, there are times when that feeling sneaks back into my mind. How can a sense of worthlessness persist for so many decades?

Through my years of therapy, I have learned that feeling worthless triggers my depression. Maybe this is how it started. Maybe it had taken root earlier and began to manifest itself at that point. I can only look back and guess. My childhood, the years before high school, are somewhat of a blur. I do not have a lot of memories. It is possible that the depression was present earlier, but currently, I do not think it matters. The depression revealed itself and no looking back on it is going to change things.

Today, the journals are safely locked up in a briefcase in my house. While I have not read the poetry I wrote as teenager in over 30 years, there is one line that I have always remembered, "i want to end this wretched life i lead." I was so young when I wrote those words. Yet they spoke so much about what the depression was doing to me. I definitely had what would now be called suicidal ideation. In other words, I was suicidal. Now when the depression gets bad, the idea behind those words return to me. When I hear those thoughts in my head, I know I need to reach out for help. I usually call Dr. Klein, my psychologist. He helps me through the suicidal ideation. At this point in my life, I have the support system to cope with those thoughts and not act on them. It does require being aware of when they first start. That way I head them off before they take too strong of a hold. I have learned coping skills that help me work through the ideation brought on by the depression.

I have often wondered why I was able to write those words but could not reach out for help. In a way, my red spiral journals were my therapists. At some point in high school, I saw a therapist or counselor. I do not remember what her title was. She was from a Catholic charitable organization, the name of which escapes me, and she would make visits to our campus. The always-smiling high school counselor referred me to her. I do not remember how many times I saw this person. I remember not liking her, not trusting her.

One vivid memory I have is her telling me that if I did not stop thinking about killing myself, she was going to put me in the hospital. Her tone was not comforting. In fact, it caused me to shut down. I stopped talking to her about how I was feeling. I did not feel safe with her. Her threat to hospitalize me had the opposite effect of what she likely intended. I thought more about ending my life. I just made sure I did not say anything to her or anyone else. I kept my thoughts secret.

There was another time that I lost any sense of safety in getting help. I had been pulled from class to see this counselor. When it was time to return to class, the period had changed, and I had to walk into another class. That teacher, an old nun, questioned me for being late. Handing her my pass, I started to walk to my seat. In front of everyone, she said, "Who signed this? I don't know this name." Red with embarrassment, I did not know what to say. I mumbled something about asking the school's head counselor. At that point I shut down. Attention, the thing I wanted least of all, had been drawn to me.

Luckily, I have now reached a point where I know that hurting myself is not the answer. Now I know I must reach out for help when those thoughts surface. Thankfully, Dr Klein has always been there to get me through those times.

My high school years were difficult. Depression consumed my teenage years. As I look back upon that time period, I realize that I went through a lot, more than any teenager should have to go through. The help was not there, but that was a different world then. Hopefully, things are different in schools today. This was the beginning of my mental health journey, a journey that has lasted throughout my life.

3

A Quiet Voice – The Humboldt State Years

The Redwood Coast

Memories of another time flood my mind;
A time when I felt peace and enjoyed much of life.
So often I long to return to that oasis among the redwood trees.
The cool air blowing in from the ocean; the scent of redwood trees summoning me back.
Memories of the time I spent under its magical scent fill me with gratitude.
Sometimes I wish I could return to the Redwood Coast;
Bring back to life the times of a quarter century ago.
I wonder if it would be the same if I returned.
The area has changed, progressed with the passage of time.
The magic of the Redwood Coast, the small-town charm may not be the same.
It is not the same just as I am not the same person.
I have lost the quietude of mind brought out by my time in the redwoods.
Those years are locked forever in my mind.
At times I close my eyes.
I see the giant redwood trees; hear the waves crashing upon the beach.
They are calling me back.
Unfortunately my life has changed.
I know I can never return to the past.
Time changes with us; prevents us from returning to a simpler life.
For now I treasure my memories; know that I cannot run away to the past.
The serenity of the Redwood Coast resides inside of me.
I need only close my eyes to call upon it.
My mind's visits are brief, but long enough to provide a sense of calm.

At some point in high school, I had to consider college. My grades were good enough to go to a California State University. There were a lot to choose from. One of the few distinct memories I have is of being in the always-smiling high school counselor's office. She asked me where I wanted to go to college. There was a poster-sized map of the California State

University system hanging on the wall next to her desk. It only took a few seconds for me to decide. After glancing at the map, I pointed to the red dot that was farthest north. It was the farthest away from Los Angeles. "I want to go to…" I read the words next to the dot. "…Humboldt State University." The counselor asked me why I had chosen Humboldt State. I think she was expecting me to say something about its programs or its reputation. "It's the farthest Cal State from Los Angeles," I replied. Little did I know then how pointing to that red dot at the northernmost point on the map would affect my life.

My decision was made in that moment. I knew I had to get away. I did not understand why. Would the darkness follow me? I had no way of knowing. Still, something told me that I had to escape. Humboldt State University would become my escape.

As I researched Humboldt State, I saw the beauty that surrounded it. Humboldt State is a small university with a strong academic reputation, and a state-school price tag. The university lies on the majestic redwood coast of Northern California. There are redwood trees surrounding the campus. These beauties are even standing tall on the campus. The Pacific Ocean can be seen from campus. All this nature had to bring something positive to my life.

Since I had been writing, I chose to apply as a journalism major. It seemed to make sense and it appeased my parents, who were questioning why I wanted to go so far away. I was not really interested in journalism, but it was writing. So, I chose journalism as a major when I applied.

High school graduation came and went. No big deal for me, except for the fact that I almost did not graduate. Evidently, you had to pass religion to graduate from a Catholic high school. At the last minute I managed to pass a class that I hated and received my diploma.

September arrived, or maybe it was late August, I do not remember. I found myself over 700 miles away from home in Humboldt County. Humboldt State University was far away in many ways, not just mileage. The university is located in Arcata, CA. That year, 1991, the population of Arcata was under 2,000. Arcata is a small town, vastly different from the city life of Southern California.

I moved into a dorm. My roommate was someone I did not know. I did not know anyone at Humboldt. Yet, somehow, I felt safe. I was surrounded by natural beauty. The pace of life was slower. This place would become my home for the next five years.

Not long after starting classes, I decided to do something that would forever change my life. I just did not know it at the time. I wanted to get involved in something. My hope was that I would find something to be happy about. Basketball had always interested me. So, one day I made my way over to Forbes Complex, the building that housed the gym. There I inquired about the women's basketball program. In minutes I found myself standing outside the women's basketball coach's office. What was I doing? I could not play basketball in high school, so college ball was not even an option. But I wanted to get involved in something. I wanted to belong somewhere. So, I knocked on the blue door and stood in the narrow hallway. The door slid open, revealing a cubicle office. Two smiling faces greeted me. Pam Martin and Carol Harrison stood in front of me. I struggled to get words out. Finally, I introduced myself. I told them I was interested in helping the team. Before I knew it, I was the team's manager.

It is hard to believe that was over 30 years ago. I was just on the phone with Pam yesterday. She had sent me some jewelry that had belonged to Carol. Pam told me that she knew Carol would want me to have something of hers. Carol passed away in 2018. Her passing was one of the most difficult deaths I have faced in life. Pam and Carol believed in me from day one and have been supporting me ever since. What started as an 18-year-old becoming their team manager has led to a lifelong friendship.

Basketball brought me a sense of belonging. It brought me happiness and a reason to live. Not long after getting involved with managing the team, I switched my major to physical education. Pam Martin became my academic advisor. She guided me through academic decisions and selecting the courses I would take. I did well in all my classes, except statistics. Math was never my thing.

My goal became to be a physical education teacher and a women's basketball coach. One issue that became apparent was my voice. I was very quiet. When I talked, it was barely above a whisper. That would never work in the gym. Pam and Carol were concerned. Being the proactive people they are, they immediately set out to solve the problem. Humboldt State is a small university, and everybody knows everyone else. They easily arranged for me to meet with a professor in the speech department to see if she could assist me in increasing the volume of my voice. This professor determined that it was not a functional problem. That was a relief, but it did not make my voice carry in the gym. Today I am still not loud, but I can project my voice in a classroom and in the gym.

Pam and Carol did not give up. One memory that sticks with me is when Carol told me it was time for me to teach a lesson in her basketball class. In her very direct way, she told me we had to find out if I could teach a class on my own. I had to have the voice to do it. I worried that I was not ready. I had been helping her with the class for a while at this point, but she wanted me to teach the whole hour on my own. Surely, Pam would talk Carol out of this "test".

I found Pam in the field house. She had just taught an archery class. I started helping her put the bows and arrows away. With tears in my eyes, I blurted out, "Carol says I have to teach her basketball class next week. What if I can't do it?" Pam, bow in hand, smiled. It was a gentle, but mischievous smile.

"I know. It was my idea," Pam responded. "You can do it. You will be fine." Then she gave me some advice. She said to go home, go into my bathroom, and turn on the shower. She told me to practice blowing my whistle sharply and shouting with a commanding voice. Shout? How was I going to do that? But as always, I did what Pam suggested.

I could not believe it was Pam's idea. Now I had no one to talk Carol out of this crazy "test". Surely, they knew I was not ready. I had not found my voice yet.

On the scheduled day, I sat on the rubber floor in the West Gym. Carol walked in. "You look green," she said with a smile. "Time to teach. Get up and blow your whistle!" My stomach clenched. I could not swallow. Carol was not going to give me a way out. I stood up and blew my whistle. There was no way out. Before I knew it, I was running the class. Carol was on the sideline, smiling. As tough as she was, I always knew when Carol was proud of me.

I spent college learning from Pam and Carol about basketball, teaching, and about life. Depression was still an issue, but I hid it well. What everyone saw as me being quiet was really me struggling with depression. Although, looking back on it, despite the depression, the five years I spent at Humboldt State were probably the happiest of my life. I had the support and love of people who I consider part of my family. Everything I have achieved professionally as a teacher, coach, and advocate stems from what I learned and developed during this time. The depression was there, but it was also different than before. It was not as all-consuming.

It was at Humboldt that I was first diagnosed with depression. Dr. H, a doctor in the student health center, recognized it and referred me to therapy. She also put me on an antidepressant for the first time. The student health center was a godsend. I was able to see doctors and counselors. I was able to get the medication I needed.

With counselors, I remember two of them, I learned to discuss what I was feeling. I learned that I had depression and was not just a sad person. Dr. H always treated me with respect. When I had my first anxiety attack, she identified it and talked to me about it. In the first few years after I graduated, I would stop by and visit with her when I was in Humboldt County. I have since learned that doctors who understand mental health are often few and far between.

One of the greatest gifts Pam and Carol gave me was a sense of belonging. That was instrumental in my mental health journey. I always knew they cared about me. I knew they wanted me to be successful. They believed in me. That did not stop when I earned my degree and left Humboldt State. When something good happens to me now, Pam is one of the first people I call. Even though she passed away, I "hear" Carol cheering me on. As much as I love Humboldt State University, it was the people I met there—Pam, Carol, and others—who made a difference in my life. The university represents all that I gained as a person from my time there. I received more than a degree. I learned life lessons and learned that I was worthy of being cared about.

It was Pam and Carol's belief in a shy, anxious college student that allowed me to become a teacher, coach, and advocate. They saw something in me. I do not know what they saw, but they allowed that piece of me to develop. I am forever grateful to them.

My Humboldt family is a part of me and their influence contributes to my advocacy work today. Without their belief in a shy, quiet college kid, I would not have the voice I have today. They nurtured my voice when it was first developing. If it were not for that nurturing, I doubt I would be able to speak so confidently today. I would not be able to stand in front of a room full of people and discuss my journey. I would not have the confidence to look at an audience and say, "My name is Gina and I have a mental illness." The nurturing and confidence I received as a college student has allowed me to share my story with others and allowed me to make a difference.

4

Depression – A Firsthand Experience

Depression

Depression hurts.
It is a silent pain,
Often hidden from others.
A smile on the outside masks the torment within my mind.
Words spin in my head.
Thoughts that will not stop create a barrage that drags me down.
No one hears these thoughts.
Others cannot comprehend the pain caused by these nagging words.
Depression is a lonely condition.
One that so often a person battles alone.
Out of fear that others will not understand, I isolate myself.
The depression gathers strength.
I worry others will notice and think I am weak.
Despite knowing the depression is real,
I fear others will belittle my affliction.
Society does not recognize the reality of depression.
People tell me to cheer up.
They do not understand that I would if I could.
There is no on-and-off switch.
I will continue to fight depression.
Some days the depression will win;
Other days I will win.
A lifelong battle with an invisible illness.
Depression hurts, depression debilitates,
But my silent battle perseveres.

Depression is difficult to explain. It can present itself in different ways for different people. There are many commonalities, but each sufferer has his or her own experience. I will describe how depression grips me. Sometimes words are not enough to explain it, but I will try.

When I speak about living with a mental illness, I am usually asked to describe depression. I have always used poetry to express what depression feels like. My poetry is an outlet for my emotions. In the early years I did not realize this, but in recent years, Dr. Klein has helped me come to the realization that I express my depression through poetry.

So how do I describe depression? Depression weighs on me like a blanket in the summer heat. When the depression is weighing on me, I have zero motivation to do anything. Negative words are hurled around in my mind, creating a thunderous noise. Just getting out of bed is a struggle. Interacting with others becomes a Herculean task. I retreat into myself.

The depression is consuming. It takes over my entire being. Depression is painful. This pain is difficult to explain because it is not a physical pain. Rather it is an all-consuming pain. I hurt on the inside. At times I think I would rather be in physical pain. To say I would rather be in physical pain is a powerful statement, but it speaks to intense emotional pain I feel as a result of depression.

Sometimes I curl up on my bed under my weighted blanket because it is the only place I feel safe. My eyes close. Tears leak out. I try to force myself to feel better, but it is futile. When I reach this point, the depression has won the battle.

Depression is invisible to the outside world. Yet it is so real. At times when I am depressed, I can still fake it. I can pretend that I am okay. This is definitely not healthy. Rather, it is a coping mechanism. Something I have learned to do to survive. I would not say that I smile, but I can manage a facial expression that hides the depression. I can act as if I am okay when in reality I am not. In all honesty, I am not sure how I do it. I have hidden the depression for so long that it is just second nature to me. It is when I cannot hide the depression that I know it is past time to reach out for help.

The word that best describes my depression is darkness, a suffocating darkness. There is no light, no way to see through the pain of the depression. Depression is darkness. It is as if the lights have been turned out on my life. Even when there are things to be happy about, depression prevents me from experiencing joy. It clamps its iron fist around me, prevents me from doing much of anything. Depression is paralyzing. When it takes control, I struggle to do even the basics of self-care.

Voices that only I can hear tell me that my life is worthless; that I have no reason to live. My mind dwells on the negative. I cannot see any hope. Even though I know I should not, I believe the voices. Let me stress that I am not hearing voices. The voices I am referring to are my own thoughts. They ring in my mind. It is like the thoughts take over. They run on a loop in my mind.

A negative reel starts spinning in my head. It repeats over and over that I am worthless; that life is not worth living. The voice on the reel tells me to give up hope. I hear these messages over and over. They become the soundtrack of my depression, a soundtrack that would ruin any movie it accompanied. This is what depression has done to my life. I am ruined, damaged goods.

I have heard this negativity for over 35 years now. Is it any wonder that I believe so much of it? This reel of negativity has been playing for a majority of my life with very little to contradict its message.

Depression often leaves me numb. The emotional pain becomes so overwhelming that I feel nothing. I become a lifeless being. Sometimes numbness is better than the pain. Even though I am paralyzed to the point of not being able to function, at least I am numb to the pain. I exist beyond the pain. As if my entire being has succumbed to relentlessness of the depression.

I am not sure a person can understand it if he or she has never experienced it. Some people say that when a person is depressed, the person is sad. That is not true. Sadness is an emotional response to an event. Webster's Dictionary defines sadness as "affected with or expressive of grief or unhappiness." Interestingly, Webster lists "depressed" as a synonym for sadness. I disagree. Depression is deeper. Depression is all-consuming. Sadness can lift when something good happens or an event changes, but depression remains. Depression is an illness, a health condition.

There have been times in my life when I was sad. It is a very different feeling. Of course, there are different levels of sadness. I can be sad when my favorite women's college basketball team loses. I was sad when a colleague passed away. These are different levels of sadness. They are legitimate feelings, but they are not depression. For me, depression usually does not have a cause. It just is.

Depression comes over me like a wave. Sometimes the wave is a ripple. Other times it is a tidal wave. When depression arrives as a ripple, I am somewhat able to handle the early stage. I can usually recognize it. That does not take away its power, but I am in a better place to cope with it. Often it will build and become more difficult to deal with as it strengthens its hold on me. Other times the depression hits like a tidal wave. Its power in these moments is overwhelming. It blindsides me. At these times I withdraw from my normal routine. I must be alone even though that probably strengthens the depression. All I can do is crawl into bed and hide in the darkness. Waiting it out seems to be my only option. In my mind, it is never going to end. Even though history tells me that it will pass when it is finished with me, I have trouble believing that.

Depression does not have a turn-off valve. When I am in the midst of depression, I cannot make it stop. There is no way to ease its grip. The more depression tightens its grip, the more I fight it. The hold depression has on me is painful and numbing at the same time. That may not make sense, but somehow it is my reality. Tears flow freely even while I stare blankly at the wall. I can sit like this for hours, barely moving. At these times I am oblivious to anything that might be going on around me.

You might ask how I can just sit there. Simply stated, I do not know. It just happens. Time passes me by. I am only vaguely aware that it is even passing. One minute I am sitting there. Two hours later, I have not moved. It is as if I am suspended in time, and nothing ever changes. It happens so often that I no longer question it. In a way I have come to accept it despite not liking it.

When I am depressed, I feel like I am looking at the world through a one-way window. I can see the world, but the world cannot see me. On the other side of the window, I see people living their lives. I see people interacting, enjoying each other. On my side of the window, I am alone. Who wants to be around someone who is depressed? I have shied away from relationships out of fear that someone will see my darkness and not want to be around me. Depression leads to loneliness. Ironically, loneliness leads to increased depression. It is an endless cycle. While the world goes on without me, I wallow in depression, trapped in a world I no longer want to be a part of.

One thing well-meaning people say that really bothers me is, "Why don't you just smile? There is so much to be happy about." They do not understand. I wish I could smile and make everything all right. Unfortunately, I cannot just switch off the depression. Oh, how I wish I could. What a miracle that would be! When the depression is in charge, I must ride it out. I cannot just snap my fingers and be okay. At times the depression is better than others. Sometimes I can cope with it. Sometimes I am paralyzed by it.

Depression is implacable. It is relentless. Depression has taken the joy out of my life. Left me wondering what my life would have been like if depression had never reared its ugly head. Would I have had different relationships? Would I have taken interpersonal risks? Would I have a family of my own? I guess I will never know.

What I know is that I wish things had been different. I wish depression had not stolen so much from me. Hindsight is 20/20. Maybe I would not like my life if it were different. Who is to say? It just would have been nice to know a world without depression as its driving force.

Work has always been difficult. I have been able to put up a solid façade. I have managed to work for about 25 years. I keep a lot hidden, pretend that everything is okay. When in fact, I am struggling to get through the day. It is a skill many of us with mental illness perfect. We learn to say, "I'm okay," with a slight smile. People believe us. They would rather believe us than admit they see our struggle. We would rather you believe that we are okay than let you know the truth. It is a matter of survival. It is also a function of stigma. Most people do not understand mental illness. They understand having the flu or a broken arm. Depression—that is something people do not even want to venture into.

Mental illness has caused me to miss work. Usually, it is just a day or two here and there. Several years ago, I had to take a two-month leave of absence and enter an outpatient program at a local hospital. I was struggling. Work had become near impossible. Outside of my sessions with Dr. Klein, I had no one to talk to about what I was feeling. I felt alone and overwhelmed.

Dr. D, my psychiatrist at the time, decided it was time to change classes of medication. That would require me to go completely off the medications I was taking for a couple weeks to get them out of my system. There was no way I could continue working unmedicated. So, from one day to the next I was taken out of work. It took a week or so to get me into a mental health outpatient program. It was weird not to work. The people I thought were my friends abandoned me. My family did not know what was going on. In essence, I was alone.

Being without medication for even that short time was hell. The depression and anxiety were horrible. Since I was not working, I had nothing to distract me until I started the outpatient program. Having too much time to think has never been good for me. During that short time period, I had too much time on my hands.

After I entered the outpatient program and started the new medication, I saw some improvement. It was a slow process. Everyone in the program had a mental illness. I had never been with a group of people with similar illnesses as mine before. It took some of the loneliness out of the illness. I learned that I was not alone. I realized that other people had struggles similar to my own. These were people I could relate to, people who could relate to me. In a way it was a comforting experience. It was also difficult because I was expected to share my thoughts and experiences, which is not something I was used to doing with anyone other than Dr. Klein, my psychologist.

There were group and individual counseling sessions every day. We had discussion sessions on self-care and managing our mental illness. There was even recreational therapy. This was a whole new world to me. It did not take long for me to feel comfortable in this setting. There was a sense of safety to it. Other people shared my experiences. We understood each other. Some days one of the counselors would take a few of us on a walk through the area surrounding the hospital. It was calming and gave me a sense of normalcy.

When my time in the program neared an end, I was worried. I was afraid to return to my work world. I was afraid I would not be able to live outside the structure of this program. The new medicine was helping, and I had learned a lot about myself during those two months. Yet, I was still afraid. Could I survive without the structure of this program? Dr. Klein thought I was ready. The counselors in the program thought I was ready. Dr. D was not as sure.

One of the last recommendations the program made was for me to consider electroconvulsive therapy (ECT). I did not know anything about ECT at that time. When I asked Dr. D about ECT, she became defensive and said she did not work with ECT, but could refer me somewhere else. At the time I trusted Dr. D. I thought she always did what was best for me. So, I put the idea of ECT out of my head. This treatment option would not resurface again until years later when I was seeing a different psychiatrist.

With depression, what people see versus what is actually happening can be tremendously different. On the outside I might look okay. At times I can pass off the depression as just being tired or overworked. I frequently use being tired as an excuse especially at work. Most people believe it and I rarely, if ever, get pressed further.

Sometimes I can even smile despite the depression. Although, that is not easy. Often, I must fake it as a teacher. I must pretend I am okay for the sake of my students. My students deserve all that I can give, but sometimes I do not have enough to give. When it is one of those days, it is better for me to take the day off and let a substitute teacher take my place. Mental health days are important. However, they come with a stigma attached. I cannot tell my principal I will be out for my mental health. Depression and anxiety are often not thought of as legitimate illnesses in the workplace. I find it better to say I have a cold or the flu. This way no one questions me or makes me feel bad for taking care of myself.

I have taken my share of mental health days over the years. I have even left work with anxiety-induced chest pain. However, I keep the mental health aspect to myself. People just do not understand how real depression and anxiety are. Pretending to be okay when in actuality I am struggling to get through the day is so difficult. I wish others understood. Sadly, it is often easier to pretend that I am okay than to try to explain something others cannot relate to.

Depression is debilitating despite its invisibility. As I have mentioned, depression and anxiety cannot always be seen on the outside. Mental illness, particularly depression, can be an invisible illness. People cannot see what is going on inside my mind. They cannot view the crushing negative thoughts that paralyze me. They cannot see the self-doubt that makes me afraid to say anything. The darkness that shrouds me is invisible to the outside world. I feel it with every fiber of my being, but nobody else can see it.

Some days the depression just takes over. It does not explain itself to me. The depression just clamps down upon me. Its vise-like grip holds me captive. I cannot escape. I am held down, unable to fight back. I become apathetic, not even wanting to fight back because it seems pointless. I have lived with depression for so long, it is hard to imagine a world without it. I have resigned myself to the fact that depression will always be a part of my life. Acceptance does not mean I like it or that I do not wish it would go away. It merely means that I have accepted that it is always going to be this way.

5

Anxiety Takes Hold

Anxiety Rising

I feel the anxiety rise in my chest,
An uneasy feeling that I cannot explain.
My thoughts start to swirl.
With closed eyes I tell myself to relax,
But the anxiety tightens its grip upon me.
My mind begins to race;
Thoughts no longer content to just swirl.
I feel the tension spread through my body.
The anxiety will not let go. It builds.
I am trapped within its grasp.
My appearance shows no clues to the anxiety mounting within me,
But inside I am losing control.
The rising anxiety becomes physical pain.
I search for an escape I will not find.
The anxiety controls me;
Clenches me in its consuming snare.

I first recognized the presence of anxiety in my life when I was around 20 years old. That is when I had my first anxiety attack. It came out of nowhere, or at least that is how it seemed.

I was working as a student assistant in the athletic department at Humboldt State University. That evening I was in the press box for my usual football game assignment of tracking yardage. It was an important game. We were playing a rival who, if I remember correctly, we had never beaten in football. Things were going as usual until late in the first half. Suddenly, I felt everything start to close in around me. The press box sounded really loud. I felt this intense desire to get away. Everything was magnifying. I did not understand what was happening, but I felt like I had to get away. In fact, all I could think about was running out the door. I had to leave. I am not sure how I made it home or what finally made this feeling stop. I knew something was wrong, but I did not know how to explain it.

I ended up missing the biggest win in the university's football history to that point. I was at home trying to figure out what the hell had just happened to me. The following Monday I went to the student health center. I do not remember if it was Dr. H or the counselor who told me that what I experienced was an anxiety attack. I think my medication was adjusted. It is hard for me to remember the details.

When I have anxiety attacks, there is a sense of being overwhelmed. Everything closes in on me and I cannot control my tears. Sometimes I can feel the anxiety building up before an anxiety attack happens. Other times they erupt out of nowhere.

For me, anxiety often makes its presence known with chest pain. Many times, I have thought I was having a heart attack, which has resulted in more than one trip to the emergency room. Tests are run. All negative. I am referred to my primary care provider each time. The emergency room doctors all send me back to my primary care provider, not my psychiatrist. That has never made sense to me. Luckily, except for one, I have had good primary care providers.

Each time I would end up in my psychiatrist's office. Dr. D, my psychiatrist for about ten years, would prescribe Ativan. Her answer was always to take Ativan. Unfortunately, one Ativan would always lead to another Ativan. One was never enough, but I did not realize this. I just kept blindly taking the pills. At one point she switched me to Xanax, but I did not like the way it made me feel and I went back to Ativan. I took the pills for years, unaware that I was addicted. Dr. D never saw a problem with this. If she did, she never told me. She just kept prescribing it. I was blind to the problem. It took more and more Ativan to control my anxiety. Looking back, I am not sure it was even helping. If it was helping, I would not have needed to take as much as I was. Dr. D never explained that to me. She just kept her prescription pad ready.

When I am anxious, everything speeds up. I feel rushed. The world closes in on me. The negative thoughts in my head intensify as if they are yelling at me. My body feels on edge. It is as if I am shaking. The chest pain starts. I lose control of everything. Just as with the depression, I want to hide from everyone and everything.

Because of the chest pain, I have had many cardiovascular tests performed to rule out my heart. The tests have been repeated at different times over the years to ensure that nothing has changed. These tests always come back normal. Except for high blood pressure, my heart is normal. That is a good thing, but it does not cure the anxiety. Knowing it is not my heart provides a sense of relief. At the same time, it reemphasizes the fact that I have a mental illness. The chest pain is real. Some doctors do not believe me, but I know what I feel. No doctor has a right to minimize what I am experiencing. My current psychiatrist, Dr. Sullivan, and Dr. Klein have helped me understand that. M, a primary care provider, was great about taking the chest pain seriously. She never minimized it. We discussed what my chest pain felt like. M explained how chest pain from a heart attack would feel. I now understand the difference, which helps me cope with the pain better.

Anxiety is difficult to live with. My mind becomes overwhelmed with negative thoughts. These thoughts like to try to predict problems. They tell me bad things are going to happen. The thoughts remind me that I am not well. Often, the thoughts scream at me. No matter how hard I try not to listen, I am overwhelmed. Imagine constantly listening to negative thoughts. It is damaging to my self-esteem. I am torn down.

Combined, the negative thoughts and the physical symptoms (chest pain, inability to be still) build up and I become paralyzed. I have to get away from whatever environment I am in, but that is not always easy to do. The anxiety often attacks when I am at work. I cannot just leave. I would never be able to tell my principal that I am having an anxiety attack and need a break. It would not go over well. Again, the stigma surrounding mental illness rears its ugly head.

I must fight through the anxiety. I have learned to use coping skills. Sometimes breathing
exercises help. Other times I use the self-hypnosis practice that Dr. Klein has taught me. Self-talk also helps. At times it is necessary to talk back to the anxiety, tell it to stop. I do that by shouting, "stop!" in my mind. I tell the thoughts that they are not in control. I tell them that they are lies. Anything to gain a bit of control. Breathing exercises, self-hypnosis, and self-talk take practice and do not always work. It is important that I engage in these strategies early in the anxiety attack. The sooner I gain control, the easier it is to stop the anxiety or at least ease it.

Oftentimes, anxiety freezes me. This is most evident in healthcare settings. I frequently freeze up when I see doctors. I have difficulty expressing myself. I can barely speak. I do not understand why this happens. I literally feel the anxiety gripping me when I am in a doctor's office. It is a physical sensation, like I am being smothered. It is better with some providers than with others. I can relax a little with my current primary care provider because she has demonstrated that she understands my mental illness and she cares enough to make sure I am at ease. Not all doctors understand mental health.

Another area in which I frequently have anxiety is in social situations. I am an introvert. I do not do well in group situations. When in a group I feel the anxiety well up inside of me. My thoughts tell me that I do not fit in with the others. They tell me I do not belong. Sometimes all the self-talk in the world is not enough to fight these thoughts. Frequently I will avoid social situations. I have improved in this area, but it is difficult for me.

When the anxiety takes control, no one notices. The anxiety causes chest pain that at times mimics the pain of a heart attack. This is all going on inside of me. No one sees it. No one understands that it is real. I know how real it is. For years I took Ativan to cope with the chest pain, to calm the anxiety. No matter how often I took a pill, the pain would come back. That led me to take pill after pill until I became addicted to Ativan. Even today, several years after overcoming the addiction, I still crave the pills at times. My mind will start telling me I need Ativan. That Ativan is the only thing that can make me feel better. It is an awful feeling to crave a medication that does nothing for me. Mental illness has done this to me. Yet so many people do not see it as a real illness.

Anxiety and depression are invisible to the outside world, but they are so real to those of us who suffer from mental illness. I struggle to comprehend how mental illness can be so misunderstood. It is so real to me. Even doctors who are supposed to understand health often do not get it. More on this in Chapter 9.

Depression on its own is difficult. Anxiety on its own is difficult. Combined, their debilitating effects are an enormous weight to bear. For me the depression and anxiety trigger each other. I rarely struggle with one without the other lurking nearby. It is as if they are co-tormentors, laughing as they wreak havoc on my life. The depression is present more often. It has been with me longer, entering my life when I was a young teenager. Its darkness wraps itself around me like a shroud. Squeezing the joy out of me; robbing me of happiness. Not to be outdone, the anxiety always wants to join the party. As I lay in bed covered in depression's darkness, the anxiety manifests through my thoughts and then the chest pain. Depression and anxiety are not satisfied with just consuming my mind; they attack my body as well.

There have been times when I have prayed for the chest pain to be my heart instead of anxiety. At these times I think it would be kinder for my heart to just take me out of my misery. I am not sure that these thoughts are actually suicidal. They are more desperate. I want the pain to cease. I want the depression and anxiety to give up the control they hold over my life.

25

When the depression has me so down that I do not care about anything, it is difficult to deal with the physical symptoms of the anxiety. At times I have sought medical attention. So often I have been met with misunderstanding. I have been dismissed by medical professionals because of my mental health diagnosis. Doctors think the pain is not real because I have an anxiety disorder. If they could only feel what I feel. Maybe then they would understand how real it is. Anxiety may be causing the pain, but the pain is real. The depression often makes me give up fighting the pain. I find myself thinking it is hopeless. I realize that no one can help me. I feel so alone. These thoughts make the depression worse. The depression then continues to trigger the anxiety, which keeps the pain going. It is an endless cycle that I am unable to break.

Living with depression and anxiety is never easy. Some days are harder than other days. Often, it seems bad days outnumber the good. Or at least it did before TMS. More on TMS in Chapter 12.

Depression and anxiety are multifaceted. They are mental and physical. They weigh me down, paralyze me. I hate it. But I understand that it is an illness. I need to confront it. I cannot stand back and let anxiety rule my life. If I did, my life would be miserable, and I would never leave my house. With the depression and anxiety, I have a battle on my hands. It is a part of my journey.

6

The Lies Alcohol Told Me

The Mud

I am hurting;
Scared and confused.
I must take flight, flee from the pain,
But it follows me.
Everywhere I turn, there it is, mocking me.
Dragging me down.
Leaving me to crawl through muddied emotions.
Stinging tears flow from my eyes.
Blinding me, preventing me from seeing clearly.
I continue to crawl, but the mud thickens.
I realize that I am trapped.
With nowhere to go and too much pain to bear,
I allow myself to sink deeper.
Soon the mud covers me.
I barely keep my head from going under.
The will to fight gives way to dejection.
Knowing I will never be free from the mud,
I continue to sink.
The pain intensifies.
Resisting the mud as it pulls me down is useless.
I will never make it back up.
The damage is done.
I am covered in mud, unable to breathe.
I give in.

As I have said, depression reared its ugly head in my life when I was a young teenager. I was not diagnosed until several years later. Writing poetry helped me get through the intervening years, but it was not enough. I needed something to make the emotional pain stop. I discovered false hope in the bottle as a teenager. I do not remember the exact night I started drinking, but at some point, the thought that alcohol could make me feel better entered my mind.

I began by mixing clear alcohol, like vodka and gin, with Dr. Pepper at night after everyone had gone to bed. No one knew I was drinking. What started as an attempt to feel less pain became an every-night activity. I slowly started using less and less Dr. Pepper. Eventually, I was drinking straight vodka and gin. I was good at hiding the fact that I was drinking. I would add water to the bottle when it got low. My parents would buy a new bottle. I was drinking myself to sleep every night, but no one knew.

Drink in hand I would climb the stairs to my bedroom, put a Grace Slick album on my turntable, and drink. I would engage in what I now know were self-harming behaviors, hitting my hand with a hammer and scraping my wrist with a kitchen knife, leaving bruises and scrapes no one asked about. These behaviors and the drinking were attempts to replace the emotional pain with physical pain. I do not know what led to it. I do not understand why I did it. I just started engaging in these behaviors. It was one of my ways of coping. These were definitely unhealthy and did nothing to bring about healing, but I was alone in my pain and did not know what to do. Today, a therapist would easily recognize the signs of depression, but I was going through this alone. Looking back on it, maybe the always-smiling high school counselor or the therapist she made me see should have noticed, should have acted. That did not happen. There is nothing I can do about it now. I can look back and ask, "What if?" But that will not change the course of my life. I have no interest in casting blame.

There were nights when I wanted to take my life. The alcohol always seemed to give me more confidence to hurt myself. Not really a healthy coping skill. I would drink until I passed out, which usually did not take long. I remember waking up some mornings and finding scribbled attempts at poems. They were illegible and the ink swerved off the page. I would go to school hung over. It did not matter. By this point school did not matter to me. Nothing mattered.

I continued drinking in various levels of intensity until I was 29 years old. It was then that an emergency room doctor told me I was going to end up dead if I kept drinking. Something made me take him seriously. I quit drinking on May 19, 2002. Recently, I celebrated 20 years of sobriety by going to brunch with my friend Sarah and her family.

You might be wondering how I quit drinking. It was not easy. Dr. Klein led the way. We discussed why I was drinking. I remember telling him that alcohol had always made it easier to cope and made life less painful. He explained that the alcohol was just masking the pain. He helped me see that alcohol was actually causing more pain even though it felt like it was relieving the pain. Masking pain does not help. It only hides the true cause. I was drinking because of the depression, but the drinking was making me more depressed. It was a vicious cycle.

Dr. Klein used cognitive behavioral therapy (CBT) to work with me. His strategies taught me to make behavioral changes to avoid the alcohol. We discussed coping skills to turn to instead of having a drink. These included going for a walk, listening to music, going to the gym, and writing. By no means was this easy. It took a lot of work. I shed a lot of tears. One day without a drink became two days. Two days became a three. Then I reached a week without a drink. We kept focusing on it. One week turned into two weeks. Marking the milestones gave me something to be proud of. Still, it was not easy.

Some nights were tougher than others. The urge to drink would pop up at different times, sometimes without warning. Even twenty years later the urge will arise, and I am forced to deal with it. I do not keep alcohol in my house. I do not let myself go to a store if I am having an urge to drink. I turn to my coping strategies. First, I try to understand why I want to the drink. Usually, it is the depression taking over. Sometimes I am anxious about something. Recognizing what the cause is allows me to work through it. I need to understand the cause of the urge so that I can give myself rational reasons why I do not need the alcohol. This helps me focus on underlying issues. I must deal with those before I can overcome the urge.

Once I have an idea of where the urge is coming from, I make a decision about how to deal with it. Sometimes distraction is the answer and listening to music helps. Sometimes I need physical activity. So, I go for a walk. Often, I listen to music as I walk. Other times I write about what is going through my head. I write poetry or journal entries. Writing gets the thoughts out of my head and onto the page. These strategies are always in my toolkit to assist me through the tough times.

Staying sober has not been easy. Even twenty years after that last sip, there are still times when I feel the urge to drink. I keep myself away from it. Usually, the urges happen when a bout of the depression is in full gear or when I get too anxious. The thought that I need a drink enters my mind. I try to ignore it, but it grows more insistent. The voice I hear is my own voice, just as the voice of the self-harming thoughts is my voice. I must tell myself it is not me. The voice is a liar. I do not need the alcohol.

There are times when the skills in my toolkit are not enough. It is in these times that I call Dr. Klein. We discuss what is causing the urge. He reminds me how often I have overcome these urges and promises that I can overcome them again. Just talking to him usually helps me calm the urge. I am then able to use one of my coping skills successfully. In this way I get through the urge to drink.

Luckily, I have learned that alcohol will not solve any problems. I know that I cannot turn to it. That would lead me down a dark, frightening path. I do not want to go there. So, I lean on Dr. Klein when I need to. I rely on my own strength. I have a few friends who have dealt with alcoholism, and I know I can turn to them for support.

Depression is an illness. I used alcohol to cope with it and developed another illness, alcoholism. In hindsight, I did not know any better. There were people who should have caught it, but they did not. I would like to believe that we are better today about catching kids before depression's grip becomes too tight, before they turn to poisonous methods to feel better. Sadly, I am not sure we are.

7

Therapy

A Lighthouse Standing Tall

For years you have guided me;
Held my emotions.
Lifted my mood and
Explained my pain.
You have allowed me to grow;
Enabled me to become myself.
Your words have counseled me
You have made sense of my anxieties and
Eased my depression.
Given me a strength I did not know I possessed.
A voice of reason in my darkened world,
You have always known just what to say.
Understood how to bring me a bit of healing.
You have been there when there was no one else;
Provided comfort with your calm demeanor.
You are always there.
A lighthouse standing tall.
A beacon of light in the darkness.

In 2002 I was working as an elementary school special education teacher. The depression and anxiety were still and issue, but I was coping by taking antidepressants and an anxiety medication prescribed by a primary care provider and drinking alcohol to numb the emotional pain. Basically, I was not in a good place, but I was doing what I do. I was surviving.

On this early spring day, I was in my classroom. My students must have been at recess because I was alone. At the time I shared a bungalow with another special education teacher. Our classrooms were connected by a common door. I found myself sitting on the floor leaning against a rolling cabinet. I do not know how I got there. I was not sure what was going on.

A fog had come over me. I am not sure how long I sat there. I looked up and standing above me was a second grader with Down syndrome. He had come through the connecting door to use the restroom, which was located in my classroom. He was smiling at me curiously. Knowing I needed help, I told the student to get his teacher. She came rushing in and asked me if I was okay. I had no idea. I was unsure how I had gotten on the floor. It felt like the world was closing in on me. My chest was hurting. Chest pain had become a common occurrence for me.

A colleague rushed me to the hospital. I was somewhat aware of what was happening. Aware enough to decline an ambulance. Once we arrived at the hospital, nurses began attending to me. The greatest concern was the chest pain. I could not possibly be having a heart attack. Women in their late 20s do not have heart attacks, do they? Well, this one was not having a heart attack. The tests on my heart all came back normal. A young doctor shared the results with me. After many questions he determined I had an anxiety attack. He asked me about alcohol. I admitted that I drank to deal with the depression. He blinked at me. Then he said if I kept it up, I was going to end up dead. I needed therapy. He referred me to my primary care provider.

Within a week I saw my primary. She made a referral for me to see a psychiatrist. I do not think I was ready for this. I had been in therapy in college and graduate school, but had been on my own for the last several years. I had never seen a psychiatrist.

In all honesty I do not remember much about that psychiatrist. I did not see her for long. I am sure she made medication changes, but I do not remember what they were. What I do remember is that she introduced me to the psychologist who would become instrumental in all of the healing I have attained since then. Her office was in the practice he owned. She wanted me to start seeing him right away.

My first appointment with Dr. Richard Klein, PhD came as I was trying to quit drinking. Little did I know then that twenty years later Dr. Klein would still be the one who guides me through the challenging times. A couple years ago I wrote a poem for him. I portrayed him as my lighthouse.

In his office I sat in a dark brown recliner across from him. Slowly, I began opening up to him. In the beginning, much of our focus was on ending my use of alcohol as a means of coping with depression and anxiety. Thinking back on that time, I do not remember much of the words. I just know that without Dr. Klein's help I would have kept drinking. Even today, twenty years later, when I feel the urge to drink, Dr. Klein helps me avoid the temptation. He is who I turn to when that urge pushes me to the edge.

Over the years he has heard me say that I need a drink many times and he has always been able to talk me out of it.

I feel safe with Dr. Klein. He listens. Often, he understands what is going on in my head more than I do. He allows me to talk through the depression and anxiety, filling in when I do not know what to say.

Dr. Klein uses some tenets of cognitive behavioral therapy (CBT) when we are in session. The purpose of this is to change my thought patterns. It also works on changing the biochemistry of my brain, which in turn would change my mood.

Therapy would not be successful if there were no behavior change leading to mood change. Dr. Klein relies on creating persistence and consistency to affect behavior change. We work on how I am responding to situations and emotions. This requires me to understand how I respond and why I respond the way I do. Working with Dr. Klein has allowed me to develop these skills. By creating a persistent effort and developing consistency, therapy results in mood change.

My depression has affected me for almost my entire life. It is lifelong depression as opposed to situational depression. Often, there is no specific trigger. The depression is just there. At these times especially, depression can be hugely debilitating. That is why I need continuous therapy. I need to work with a psychologist. Starting and stopping therapy would not work for me. I need the continuous support of someone who understands my depression and how I respond to it. Therapy allows me to feel secure. It gives me the space to process the depression.

Dr. Klein has provided me with many strategies over the years to cope with my mental illness. Developing the ability to discuss what I am feeling is one of the greatest gifts he has given me. When we talk, he guides me toward a better understanding of what I am thinking and feeling. I developed the skills to process what the depression and anxiety do to me. Of course, there are times when it is still overwhelming. At some points the depression and anxiety become too much for me. This is when having Dr. Klein is instrumental. Like a lighthouse standing tall in the ocean of mental illness, he lights my path.

A self-care strategy that Dr. Klein introduced me to is self-hypnosis. Pre-pandemic, we ended all of our sessions with this technique. I reclined in the chair and closed my eyes. Dr. Klein's voice then guided me into a place of relaxation. His voice was always soft and reassuring. He led me through the progressive relaxation of my entire body. Once I was completely relaxed and in the hypnotic state, Dr. Klein spoke about whatever he wanted me to focus on, fixating my mind on healing. He gave hypnotic suggestions, like,

"You are stronger than the depression," and, "You are making decisions that put your needs first." Then, slowly, he brought me out of the hypnotic state. I rarely wanted to leave the hypnotic state. It felt so safe.

Dr. Klein taught me how to guide myself through this self-hypnosis. On many occasions it has brought me relief and a sense of peace. I rarely reach the same sense of safety on my own that I feel when he guides me through it, but it helps me, nonetheless. Self-hypnosis has become a tool in my self-care repertoire.

Dr. Klein has assisted me in seeing my mental illness for what it is, an illness. He has helped me understand that I am not at fault for having depression and anxiety. When we talk, he helps me see the depression and anxiety through a different lens. These disorders are not something I can control on my own. I need consistent therapy. I benefit from speaking with a psychologist who is familiar with me and who understands how my mental illness impacts me. It is that relationship that has led to me being able to accept this mental illness. Without that acceptance, I would not have found the healing I have found.

Writing poetry has always been healing for me, as I discussed earlier. It has been a form of therapy for me. Cathartic. It only makes sense that the first person I shared that poetry with was Dr. Klein. Over the years, he has read many of my poems. Maybe more than he has wanted to, but he always reads them. The poems make sense out of what I am experiencing. Sharing these poems has allowed us to unpack my depression and anxiety at a deeper level. That has been healing for me and taken therapy to a deeper level.

Of course, when I first started thinking about attempting to publish my poetry, Dr. Klein was right there supporting me. He has perhaps been my greatest cheerleader as I have published my books of poetry. He understands the healing qualities writing has for me. He taught me that my writing can help others, too, whether it is through knowing they are not alone in battling mental illness or in understanding the battles others face. Dr. Klein encouraged me every step of the way. When I doubted myself, he believed in me. Is it any surprise that he has received the first copy of each of my books?

I remember giving him a spiralbound draft of Cognizant Introspection, which would become my first published book. I knew he was proud of me. His encouragement led me to take the risk of self-publishing. Now I have four published poetry books on the topic of mental health. It is hard to believe that that spiralbound dream has grown into four books, numerous poetry readings, and many mental health talks.

The poetry readings and mental health talks have been another byproduct of Dr. Klein's encouragement. I started with poetry readings where I would share a couple poems. From there I progressed to being the feature poet at bookstore events. Eventually, I hosted my own events. I have transitioned into using my poetry as a part of discussions on mental health. I have spoken at in-person events and events live on the internet. During these events I share my journey of living with mental illness and how I have found healing. I try to let others with mental illness know they are not alone. I also try to help people who do not live with mental illness gain a better understanding of what life is like for those of us who do.

Writing about Dr. Klein is difficult. My goal was for this chapter to come out perfectly. I want readers to recognize the influence he has had on my life. Without him, I would never have made it through the last twenty years. He is my lighthouse standing tall amongst the turbulent waves of my depression and anxiety; a steadying voice in the torrent of mental illness.

8

A PA Steps In

A Simple Question

You asked a question when I thought no one cared.
As you awaited my response I saw the look in your eyes.
You really wanted to know my answer.
You cared when no one else did.
My reply was simple,
But you heard so much more.
The answer I gave was not enough.
You wanted to know more; to really understand.
So you coaxed and you prodded.
I did not know anything was wrong until you explained.
With heartfelt words and keen understanding you took me in,
Enabled me to understand.
In that moment you changed my life.
You started my healing with one simple question.
Opened my eyes and
Gave me hope.
Today I reflect back on that moment.
I wonder if you know what a difference you made.
You stepped in when no one else could.
I am forever grateful that you took the time to ask a question
And listened for my answer.
You went beyond your role and made a difference.

Late in 2015, it became difficult to work. I was having anxiety attacks more frequently. The chest pain was almost constant. To deal with it, I was taking Ativan several times a day. It was easy to get. As I discussed earlier, the psychiatrist I was seeing at the time, Dr. D, would prescribe as much as I needed. Ativan would ease the chest pain caused by my anxiety, but only for a short time. People at work noticed that I was not okay, but no one was saying anything directly to me.

36

I was seeing Dr. D monthly. She kept prescribing pills. Nothing seemed to help, but her answer was always that a new pill or dosage change would help. I believed her. I had been seeing her for about ten years. I had no reason not to believe her.

Our conversations typically went like this:

Dr. D: "How are you doing today?"

Me: "The same."

Dr. D: "Let me check what you are taking?" Glances at her computer. "Let's increase this medication and try this one."

Me: (taking a prescription slip) "Okay."

Dr. D: "I'll see you in a month."

There was probably more to the conversations, but this was the main gist of them.

Chest pain had become a constant reminder of my anxiety. I experienced it daily. One afternoon, when my chest pain was particularly bad, I had an appointment with my primary care provider, a physician's assistant named M. I was shaking as she stood in front of me in the exam room. M was very familiar with my depression and anxiety. I had been seeing her for a couple of years at this point. She had always been understanding about my mental illness. She always asked how I was coping with the depression and anxiety. She knew about the chest pain and had ordered a few EKGs, all of which had come back normal.

On this day M asked me a question that changed my life. It marked a new step on my journey toward true healing. We had been talking about the chest pain. Then she asked a simple question. "Why are you taking Ativan that way?" I did not understand her question. I looked at her, blinked. I will never forget the expression on her face. It was a mixture of care and confusion.

I replied with the only answer I had. "Because that's what my psychiatrist tells me to do." The look on her face did not change.

"But that's not how you are supposed to take it." M's response left me speechless. What was she talking about? I was taking it the way Dr. D prescribed. M explained that I should not be taking it as often as I was and that it was not supposed to be taken nightly in addition to "as needed". I stared at her for a beat.

Until that moment it had never occurred to me to question Dr. D. Now I did not know what to think. Should I believe M? She was not a psychiatrist. She was a physician's assistant. Dr. D was a psychiatrist and had been treating my mental illness for a long time. Dr. D should know what I needed. Shouldn't she?

But something was not right. Again, I looked at M, a physician's assistant. She was not even a doctor, let alone a psychiatrist. M did not let up. She asked me about my other medications. It was difficult to keep track of how many I was on at the time. I was a walking pharmacy. M said she felt we really needed to discuss my medication use. Something told me she was right. Even today, I cannot explain what told me to trust her, but I am grateful that I did.

She scheduled me to come back the following week with all my prescriptions for a medication check. At that appointment we went through everything I was taking. I had not realized how much I was actually taking until that day. M questioned each medication. She looked up each prescription. We talked about why I was taking each one. All I knew was that the pills were for either depression, anxiety, or sleep. There was even one to wake me up. M thought I was overmedicated. She told me that it did not makes sense that I was taking so many medications.

It took me a few minutes to process this. At some level I knew she was right, which left me with many questions. Was Dr. D overmedicating me? If she was, what was I going to do? Was M right? Who should I trust?

M was reassuring. She said she could help me stop taking some of these medications. Then she explained "tapering off" to me. Tapering off is the process of slowly going off of a medication to avoid withdrawal effects.

On the surface, trusting a family care physician's assistant over an experienced psychiatrist did not make sense. But the more I thought about it, the more I heard the concern in M's voice, the more I knew M was right. In that moment I made the decision that I was going to trust M. I had been on these medications or various combinations of them for years and I was not getting better. Maybe it was time to listen to someone else.

M set up a plan to taper me off some of the medications. We also talked about my use of Ativan. I was overusing Ativan, maybe even addicted to it. It was not healthy.

I had to decide what to do about Dr. D. How could I keep seeing her? She would not be happy that I decided to listen to a physician's assistant instead of her. I could picture Dr. D's reaction. It would not be good. Dr. D could get defensive. What was I going to tell her? I needed a psychiatrist, but I realized that Dr. D had not been helping me. Still, I had been seeing her for ten years. How could I just change psychiatrists? I asked M what I should do. She told me that I did not owe Dr. D anything. We decided that I would buy some time by canceling my next appointment and then get a list of psychiatrists from my insurance company.

As I was tapering off the medications, I noticed I felt different. A fog was lifting. I had not even realized the fog had been there and here it was, lifting. The depression and anxiety were still there, but I felt like I was more alive than I had been. Was this really happening because I stopped taking so many of the medications?

It was a difficult process, especially with Ativan. I constantly felt like I needed it. I was used to taking it several times a day. Often, I would automatically reach for the bottle of little white pills without even thinking about it. I was learning to cope without it. It was not easy, but M helped me realize that I did not need to rely on pills to make me better.

Often, medication is the first option in treating depression and anxiety. I have since learned

that there are other options. More on other options in Chapter 11.

My insurance company emailed me a list of psychiatrists. I took the list to Dr. Klein. He talked to a psychiatrist that he worked with, and I began seeing that one. It was only going to be a temporary thing. I had seen this doctor years earlier, before Dr. D. I had switched to Dr. D because she was female. Dr. Klein and I then spent time searching for the right psychiatrist for me.

Before I move on, I want to reflect on M's impact. She changed my life. She freed me from overmedication. Even though she could very easily have told me to just trust my psychiatrist, she did not. It would have been easy for her to dismiss my mental health as another provider's responsibility. Instead, she listened to me. Not only to what I was saying, but to what I was not saying. She trusted her instincts as a medical professional. And, she saved me. Hindsight is obviously 20/20 but getting off those medications was a key step in my healing journey.

I should give myself some credit, too. It took courage to trust a family care physician's assistant over a psychiatrist. I am grateful for M's care. I can never repay her. Luckily, she never expected me to.

9

Ignorance in the Healthcare Field

Do You Really See Me?

I get it.
I have a mental health disorder.
You do not understand.
I see you standing there in your white lab coat.
I guess you think that I am crazy.
It is easier for you to just assume that I am my mental health.
You do not see the person behind the label.
The person who feels so deeply, who longs for life to be different.
That is who I really am.
I am not just "depressed with catatonic features".
I am more than an anxiety disorder.
I have dreams just like you.
I feel pain just like you.
Do you see me?
We are not that different.
One day you may struggle with this darkness, although I hope that you do not.
I do not wish depression on anyone.
Sometimes I wish I could better explain what it feels like to live with a mental health disorder.
Let others know what is like to see darkness all around me.
I hide my tears, wear a fake smile just to get through the day.
You only see a part of me.
Deep inside I am longing to emerge from behind my diagnosis;
Shatter the label and be seen.

Over the years I have seen many healthcare practitioners. Some understand mental health. Others do not quite get it. Still others are ignorant. It is the ignorant ones who make living with mental illness more difficult.

I was lucky to have M as my primary care provider for a few years. Change is inevitable and eventually M moved on from the clinic I go to for primary care. She recommended a colleague, E, who she said would take good care of me. I trusted M. So even though I knew things would never be the same, I was okay with moving on to a new provider. Little did I know that a life-changing incident awaited me.

The first time I saw E was after a follow-up with the cardiologist, who I was seeing for my chest pain. Going to a cardiologist was overwhelming and I always left more confused than when I arrived. At these times I would see M and she would help me make sense of whatever the cardiologist had said. So, it made sense that I would make an appointment with the primary care provider I would now be seeing. At this first appointment, E, another physician's assistant, seemed understanding. She explained what the cardiologist had said in terms I could process.

When it came time for my physical exam, I made an appointment to see E. This appointment would prove to be the most hurtful medical appointment I have ever experienced. There was no physical pain, but it was painful, nonetheless. Emotional pain lasts longer and cuts deeper than physical pain.

A little background is necessary. My anxiety often makes being in a doctor's office difficult for me. Being touched is uncomfortable for me. There is one exam that I have never been able to get through despite yearly attempts. Each attempt ends in an anxiety attack. I have tried anxiety medication, meditation, and visualization to get through this exam. Nothing has ever worked. M had come the closest to completing it, but even with her, I had anxiety attacks. Dr. Klein and M had both agreed that it was medically necessary for me to keep trying. So, I went into this appointment ready to try again.

As I waited in the exam room, I was anxious. I had a bottle of Ativan ready. When E came into the room she started with the routine parts of the physical exam. Then it was time for "the exam". I was sure she could see the failed attempts in my chart. Even though it was tough for me to clearly say it, I told her that I usually have anxiety attacks during this exam, but that I was ready to try again. I was unprepared for her next words. She told me that she would not do it. I did not understand. Then came the words that would have a major impact on me. E said, "You are a liability."

She did not say "it would be a liability to do the exam." She said I WAS THE LIABILITY. I was dumbfounded. No one had ever been that cruel before. She said it so matter-of-factly. End of discussion. I could not even respond. She said something about a referral. I did not hear her. I was trying to process being called a liability. How could a medical professional say I was a liability? I have a mental illness. I do not decide to have anxiety attacks. The attacks just happen. No harm ever came when the exam had been attempted in the past. The practitioner would always simply stop when the anxiety attack reached the point that she could continue.

I did not know what to say or do. I wanted to get out of that exam room. I wanted to run away. I wanted to scream, "I am not a liability!" But maybe she was right. The thought that it was my fault erupted into my consciousness. She seemed unfazed by her words and moved on. She told me to lie down on the table. She was going to do a breast exam. As I said, I am uncomfortable being touched. My body jumps when I am touched. In my mind I needed to warn her about this. My anxiety had already made her call me a liability. I did not want her to think that I was jumpy because she was hurting me. I meekly told her that sometimes I jump when I am touched. I am not sure what I expected her response to be. Certainly, not the response I received.

Sarcastically, she snapped, "I can't examine you if I can't touch you." She had misunderstood me. I had not been clear. I just wanted to warn her and let her know she was not hurting me. Again, I wanted to run from the room, but only a paper gown covered me from the waist up. I was trapped. She continued with the breast exam. I was so uncomfortable. I fought back tears. I unsuccessfully tried to keep my body from jumping. I needed to get out of that room. It seemed like forever before I was able to leave.

Once I was safely in my car, the tears flowed. A medical appointment was not supposed to be like that. Was I at fault? Why do I have to have a mental illness? I cried all the way home.

In the next day or two I talked to Dr. Klein. I told him what had happened. I asked him what I had done wrong. He was angry. He told me E had no right to talk to me that way. Dr. Klein assured me that my anxiety was not my fault. It was difficult for me to process. E had humiliated me. She made my mental illness my fault. Did she realize how hurtful her words were? Did she even care?

It took Dr. Klein a couple weeks to convince me that I had to complain. He told me that I could not just let her treat me that way. I decided that I was never going back to that clinic again. Following Dr. Klein's advice, I became determined to make it known why. After appointments, I always received an email from the clinic asking for feedback. Late one afternoon about two weeks after the appointment, I responded that because of the PA I saw I would never go back there again. I figured that was it. The next day I received a phone call from a woman in the clinic office asking what had happened. It was difficult, but I told her about E calling me a liability. We talked for a few minutes. I told this woman how hurtful it was. The woman was kind, but I was not at a point in my life where I could discuss the mental health aspects of this event. The woman thought I was upset about E's word choice. She apologized and told me she would let the doctor know what had happened. Then she asked me if she could convince me to stay. I hesitated. She promised me that there was another PA, who she knew would take better care of me. I reluctantly agreed.

That phone call was it. I never received an apology from E. No acknowledgment from her that her words had been hurtful. I guess I should not be surprised.

The new PA, Greta Vines Douglas, turned out to be great. She was kind and empathetic. She never made me feel at fault for my mental illness. It took some time, but Greta restored my faith in healthcare professionals.

Even today, several years later, I am haunted by E's words. Sometimes when I go into that medical clinic, I still hear her words echoing in my head. I am not sure if I will ever be completely rid of her words. It is difficult to understand how four words can be so hurtful and lasting. Often, I wonder if she ever had any clue as to how her words affected me. Has she said similar words to other patients? I find it hard to believe that I am the only victim of her ignorance. My guess is she has no idea. Even now, I sometimes wish I could confront her; hold her accountable for her words. Medical professionals are supposed to know better. They should be empathetic toward mental health. At the very least they should be aware of how they impact patients.

The impact of E's words did not end with that call from the clinic. After some time had passed, a change occurred in me. Eventually, I realized E had no right to blame me for my mental illness. Her words hurt me, but with time they also transformed me. I knew I had to advocate for my own mental health. That led me into advocating for better mental health care for others and has allowed me to join the fight to end mental health stigma. Maybe I should be grateful to E for that. In some ways I have forgiven her. However, I will never forget the pain she caused.

That pain is my inspiration for using my voice. I transformed my writing from being focused on the literary aspects of poetry to mental health advocacy. This is a change I believe I was meant to make. It a change that I am happy with. E's hurtful words led to this change. Perhaps I was meant to go through this experience so that I could find my voice as a mental health advocate.

10

A New Psychiatrist Brings Hope

Heard

Calming words spoken with sincerity greet me.
A genuine interest in what I have to say,
Allowing me to feel at ease
And open up.
I have never trusted more than I do now.
No longer a mere bystander, I am a part of my healing.
My words are heard.
My thoughts are valued.
Questions intended to truly understand how I am doing guide our conversations.
Advice is given, but never preached.
It is safe to admit when I am not okay.
My thoughts are acknowledged;
My illness understood.
Guiding me on the road to healing,
A compassionate voice has restored my hope.

Over the years I have seen a few psychiatrists. Six to be exact. One of those I have returned to between seeing other psychiatrists because he will always fill prescriptions without asking too many questions. The psychiatrist I was with the longest was Dr. D. I saw her for about 10 years and trusted her. It was not until I realized that she was overmedicating me without helping me that I knew I had to move on. That was a difficult decision, as I discussed in Chapter 8.

For a while I bounced around looking for the right psychiatrist. The first Dr. A was great, not a pill-pusher. I was with him for a little over a year until he moved his practice and I had to move on to a new psychiatrist. It would be another psychiatrist named Dr. A. In the beginning he was okay, but I never felt connected to him. Soon he began pushing me to have electroconvulsive therapy (ECT) done. This was not something I was willing to try. To be completely honest, it scared me. I read about it and listened to his explanations, but I just did not feel comfortable with it as a treatment. I was afraid of the anesthesia, the seizures—even if they were controlled—and the potential for memory loss. Dr. A kept pushing it. I did not understand why he was so insistent. As a result, I decided to find a new psychiatrist. I am not dismissing ECT as a treatment option for mental illness. It just was not the right option for me.

I called my insurance company and asked for an updated list of psychiatrists they would cover. The list arrived by email. I was not looking forward to trying to find a new psychiatrist, but I had to do it. As I went through the list, I would look a name up online. One of the first profiles I found was Dr. Sullivan. This may sound strange, but when I read her Psychology Today profile, I felt a connection. I cannot explain it. Something told me that this was the psychiatrist I needed to try. Looking back, I know that intuition was right. I have been seeing Dr. Sullivan for a few years as of this writing, and I have never felt more comfortable with a psychiatrist than I do now.

Connection to the members of your mental health team is a key to healing. I have that connection with Dr. Sullivan. I know that I am treated with respect and as an instrumental part of my own treatment. Dr. Sullivan talks with me, not at me. That was new to me. The first Dr. A was somewhat like that, but no other psychiatrist has ever treated me as if I were a part of the decision-making. I wrote a poem titled "Heard" about Dr. Sullivan.

With Dr. Sullivan I can be open. I can ask questions. We discuss how I am doing. With other psychiatrists, it was usually "how are you feeling?... Okay, let's increase this medication and will add this medication." Then it was, "see you in a month." There was no real discussion. Everything felt so rushed. The other psychiatrists never talked to me about what I was feeling. They never went below the surface. The answer to everything was a pill. Most of the time I did not know why I was taking the pills they prescribed. I could ramble off the names of the medications, but I did not know which were for depression, which were for anxiety, and which were for sleep. That was not healthy. Nor was it a productive way to deal with my mental health. The issues were just being masked.

Dr. Sullivan is different. She asks deeper questions. She listens to my answers. We discuss what I am experiencing. There is no prescription pad at the ready like with my previous psychiatrists. If she makes a medication change, she explains it to me. She checks to see if I am okay with the change. Seeing her has made such a difference for me. I feel like I have really improved as a result.

Dr. Sullivan was the first psychiatrist to recognize that I had treatment-resistant depression. She explained that medications were not helping me. One of the things I value about Dr. Sullivan is that she does not push medications the way so many other psychiatrists do. She is not constantly changing or modifying prescriptions. She talks with me. She listens to what I have to say. I truly believe that she recognizes that I understand my mental illness. She values my contribution to our discussions. In doing so, she has allowed me the space to heal.

Knowing that medication was not the answer, we discussed treatment options. She listened when I told her about my experience with the second Dr. A pushing ECT. She accepted that I did not want to try to that treatment. Her understanding made it easier for me to be open to other options. When she explained transcranial magnetic stimulation (TMS), I was willing to listen. I credit Dr. Sullivan with finding the treatment option that has worked best for me.

I feel a sense of safety with her that I have never experienced with other psychiatrists. I am part of my healing with her. She will never force me into something I do not want to do. When I need her, she is there. Dr. Sullivan is everything I have always needed in a psychiatrist.

11
Searching for Other Options

Lights

I will try to be positive.
Attempt to focus on the lights in my life.
It is so difficult
But I know I must try.
I am struggling;
Losing my hold on life.
I cannot let go.
There are lights.
I know they are within my reach.
If only I could stretch out my arm,
Grab hold and cling to one.
I will focus on just one light at a time;
Be positive for a moment.
Maybe if I can focus for just one moment,
I will find there are more lights within my reach.
Grasping, I may find enough light to brighten my life.
Be positive.
I say the words over and over again.
Allow myself to hear the words.
Positive thoughts will lead to the lights.

In 2019 my depression and anxiety became very difficult to deal with on a daily basis. I was frustrated. I felt like I could no longer handle it. Dr. Sullivan explained to me that my depression was treatment resistant. I had been on so many different medications, but none of them were ever effective enough. This scared me. As always Dr. Sullivan was straightforward yet reassuring. She explained that there were other options. It comforted me to know I had choices.

With my new understanding of treatment-resistant depression, I was able to begin researching different treatment options available to me. I discussed these with Dr. Klein and Dr. Sullivan. One option we investigated was ketamine treatment. I was open to this, but hesitant. Ketamine treatment involves taking an infusion of what I kept thinking of as a street drug. Of course, I knew from researching it, that it was not the street drug, ecstasy, but its source brought images of the 60s acid trips and hallucinations I remembered hearing about as a teenager fascinated by hippie music. Grace Slick's (of the Jefferson Airplane) lyric, "Feed your head," kept popping into my mind.

Could I really try this treatment? I was not sure. I read articles about the benefits people who were being treated with ketamine were experiencing. Dr. Klein read about it and shared what he learned with me. But the same image kept returning to my mind. I saw myself sitting in a chair with an IV inserted into my arm. Ketamine dripping from a plastic bag hanging next to me. I saw distorted, red and black geometric figures floating around me. The head of a monster jumping out at me. Swirling colors. This is how I imagined an acid trip. It is what I pictured ketamine causing.

How could this make the depression go away? Would "tripping"—hallucinating—be worse than the darkness of the depression and anxiety? I had no way of knowing. Was I brave enough to find out?

After a lot of thought, I decided not to pursue ketamine treatment at that point. It was still an option. I just was not ready to go down that path.

I also knew that electroconvulsive therapy (ECT) was not a treatment that I wanted to even consider. It had been recommended for me several years ago when I was in the outpatient treatment program. The second Dr. A had tried to get me to undergo ECT, but it scared me. I did not like the idea of being put under anesthesia for treatment. The idea of having a seizure scared me even if it was controlled by a doctor. The negative effect on memory was a side effect I did not want to deal with, either. My grandmother had Alzheimer's and my great-grandmother likely had it. I figured that I did not need to do anything that caused me to lose memories when family members suffered from Alzheimer's disease. This may not have been a solid rationale, but it is where my thoughts went. I probably could have listened to what the psychiatrist had to say about ECT. I could have researched it more on my own. The bottom line was that I was not comfortable with it. The more this psychiatrist pushed it, the more I resisted.

When Dr. Sullivan suggested that we investigate the possibility of transcranial magnetic stimulation (TMS), I felt that it was worth looking into. The difference between her suggestion and the previous psychiatrist pushing ECT was in their approaches. Dr. Sullivan never pushed it. Her approach was much gentler. She never acted like she had all the answers. We had discussions about the positives and negatives of TMS. She gave me contact information for SoCal TMS, a group she was familiar with. I felt like my concerns and fears were being listened to and that we were a team in the approach to my treatment.

The decision to try TMS was not an easy one to make. Dr. Sullivan and I spent time discussing it. I was fearful of the potential side effects, even though I did not know what they might be. I did not know what to expect. The unknown can be a frightening place, especially when you feel depressed to the point of barely functioning. I wondered if it was better to just continue to deal with the darkness of depression and anxiety, which I knew so well. There is a strange sense of safety in the known.

After that appointment I sat in my car in the parking lot and called SoCal TMS. That call led to a life-changing treatment. I spoke with a very kind intake person. She sent me paperwork to fill out and told me I needed my primary care provider to refer me. She also set up an appointment for me.

Going to my primary care provider made me nervous. It seemed strange that my psychiatrist was not the person they wanted the referral from. At the time I had just switched to a new primary care provider. Greta, who I was comfortable with, had just moved on to another position. That was difficult enough for me, but the thought of talking to a new provider about my mental health scared me. Having had negative experiences with medical professionals because of my mental health has left me tentative around them. Greta had assured me that the PA she was leaving me with was good and that she would take care of me. I wanted to believe her, but I had believed M when she told me that I could trust E and M was very wrong.

I made an appointment to see my new primary care provider, Cristina Rosales, a physician's assistant. On the day of the appointment, my anxiety was very high. How was I going to ask a PA I did not know and who did not know about my history of depression and anxiety to refer me for a non-traditional treatment? Would she even know what TMS was? Would she question me? Would she make me prove that I had depression? Prove how anxious I am?

I did not think I would be able to make sense when I went in to see her. So I wrote down notes and printed out information on TMS. I had both Dr. Klein and Dr. Sullivan's cards with me. Sometimes mental illness takes over my thinking and I become convinced that the worst will happen.

As it turned out, I did not have anything to worry about. When Cristina came into the exam room, I managed to say that I needed a referral for

TMS. She responded kindly and asked what was going on. She did not question how depressed or anxious I was like I had feared she would. Cristina looked at the TMS paperwork I handed her with a shaking hand. Then she told me she would make the referral. I remember not knowing what to say. Here was a PA who I had never seen before, who did not know how bad my depression and anxiety were. Yet she was willing to trust me when I said that my psychiatrist and I felt I needed TMS.

Now I had everything I needed to try TMS. I also took a step toward trusting my new primary care provider.

12

What is TMS?

Healing

Full of doubt and without hope I entered.
Figuring I would go through another useless attempt to heal,
but not really believing.
I was met with positivity, friendly faces who did not push too hard.
Instead they welcomed me.
Explained what they were going to do;
Reassured me.

Transcranial magnetic stimulation, TMS, sounds like something out of a sci-fi movie.
A machine seems a big leap from a bottle of pills and a stack of medicated patches.

Somehow the doctor persuaded me to give it a try.
The techs built trust with their caring words and gentle touch.
Always checking on me, making sure I was okay.

I sat there wondering what I was doing.
A magnetic device attached to my head.
Pulsating pokes somehow lifting the depression, taming the anxiety.
I wondered, could this device really work?
Is it really making a difference?

After 30 years of struggling with depression I never thought I could find healing;
discover new hope in my life.
But TMS has given me just that.

Goodbye, depression, once my sole companion.
Good riddance, anxiety, once the tormentor of my mind and body.
Thank you, TMS, for giving me a new chance to truly experience life.

Since transcranial magnetic stimulation (TMS) has been such an integral part of my healing, I would be remiss if I did not explain it. I had a very basic understanding of the treatment as I underwent it, but to do it justice I needed more. Stephanie Debnath, PMHNP-BC, graciously sat down with me to discuss TMS. She is the psychiatric nurse practitioner who oversees my treatment at SoCal TMS Center in Pasadena, CA, which is directed by Dr. Todd M. Hutton, MD FAPA, a pioneer in the field.

Transcranial magnetic stimulation is an FDA-approved treatment for major depression. It is a safe, effective, and noninvasive treatment for patients who have not experienced relief from more traditional treatments such as medication. Knowledge of TMS has existed for over 100 years and has been studied for the past 35 years. The FDA gave its approval for TMS to be used to treat major depression in 2008. Initially, TMS providers had to appeal multiple denials to get insurance companies to approve treatment. In 2011, insurance coverage became available. Now, most insurance companies cover it as a treatment for major depression.

TMS is a magnetic resonance imaging (MRI)-based technology. It utilizes the same magnetic coil that can be found within an MRI bed. During TMS treatment, the magnetic coil is enclosed in a casing with a slight contour that rests gently toward the front of the patient's skull. I did not experience any discomfort during treatment. I could feel something resting on my head and, of course, I felt the pulses, but I was comfortable during treatment.

So how does this treatment work? Stephanie explained that TMS uses magnetic pulses to induce an electrical current in the patient's brain. This takes advantage of the electrochemical nature of the brain. TMS forces the brain to fire at a much higher rate than it is used to. The purpose of this is to increase the activity in certain regions of the brain that may be underactive. TMS targets the dorsolateral prefrontal cortex (DLPFC), which drives the mesolimbic pathway. The mesolimbic pathway is the brain's mood center. As the DLPFC is forced to fire, it is being trained to connect more effectively with the rest of the brain. This is an attempt to stimulate a lobe that is not optimally communicating with the rest of the brain. The brain is being trained to have all its circuitry connect. Stephanie described it as giving the brain a "jumpstart".

TMS requires a series of treatments. In my case, 38 sessions were required each of the four times I have undergone this treatment. Each session lasted about 50 minutes. During that time, I would watch television. I binged watched shows like Schitt's Creek, Golden Girls, and New Girl. As my symptoms improved, I was also able to engage in conversations with the nurses and techs who oversee the treatment. I became more socially aware and able.

According to SoCal TMS Center, a typical TMS session lasts 30-60 minutes and is provided five days a week (Monday through Friday). During treatment the patient is awake and alert. The patient is reclined in a chair set to the patient's comfort. The nurses/techs prepare the correct settings for the patient. They ask a few routine questions to establish how the patient is doing.

Before the start of each daily treatment the nurse would ask me to rate my depression and anxiety on a scale of one to 10. This allowed them to track my daily progress. Then the treatment begins. No effort is required on my part. I felt the tapping of the pulses, but experienced no pain.

While treatment is in progress, the patient is free to watch TV or listen to music. 30-minute comedies worked for me because when I need treatment, my ability to concentrate is not that great and I can only follow a television show for short periods of time.

Once a week a psychiatrist or psychiatric nurse practitioner meets with the patient. Stephanie met with me. She asked about my mood, looking for subtle changes that even I might miss. It often takes an outside eye to notice the changes in the beginning. She ensured that I was tolerating the treatment well. These check-ins made me feel more secure. I felt like I was being cared for, not just given treatment.

These check-ins were in addition to my weekly therapy sessions with Dr. Klein and my normal sessions with Dr. Sullivan. SoCal TMS keeps the patient's psychiatrist and therapist updated on treatment. This team approach allowed me to feel like I mattered. Suffering from depression is often a very solitary battle. Having a team of care providers eases that aloneness.

I have experienced the benefits of TMS firsthand. Remission of symptoms has been the greatest benefit. Each time the remission has lasted for several months. Before TMS I did not know that it was possible to not feel depressed. Now I am better able to understand my depression because I can distinguish the difference between being depressed and not being depressed. It is an amazing difference. A weight has been lifted off me. I do not feel like I am shrouded in darkness. I am not sure I can even explain it. More on this in Chapter 15.

Stephanie shared that some patients tell her, "I don't feel like I am my depression anymore." The depression is no longer who they are. They are more aware. I can attest to this feeling. The awareness I have gained has allowed me to function better. My psychologist, Dr. Klein, has noted this change in our sessions. Now when I am depressed or anxious, I am better able to explain where it is coming from or what is causing it.

When I discussed this with Stephanie, she told me that "depression is less like a broken bone and more like diabetes." I immediately understood. Depression and anxiety are chronic illnesses. Sufferers learn to live with the illness, but that does not make it any easier. We must learn to manage it and keep it away. That requires people with mental health disorders to stay on top of the illness. TMS provides the help needed to keep ahead of depression and anxiety.

Each of the times I have undergone TMS treatment, the improvement in my mood has started to occur in about the third week. The improvements came on slowly. It started with being able to get myself out of bed without battling the desire to stay under the covers. I felt lighter. Slowly I started to feel like I could be more a part of the world around me. The sense of darkness that shrouds me when the depression is in control lifts. It is difficult to explain how this happens, but it does happen. I may not be able to explain it, but I will take it. It is an incredible feeling.

SoCal TMS Center states that the benefits of TMS can vary because of the different symptoms and severity of a patient's depression. TMS is noninvasive. The encased coil is on the surface of the skull. TMS is also non-systemic, meaning that it does not have to go throughout the body like medication does. Unlike ECT, TMS does not require hospitalization, anesthesia, or IV medications. TMS also does not cause memory loss which is often experienced with ECT.

After each treatment the patient can go about their daily routine. I was able to drive myself to and from treatment. Several of my treatments were done early in the morning so that I could go to work afterward.

I did not experience any significant side effects from treatment. SoCal TMS Center identifies headaches, sensitivity at the treatment location, and fatigue as possible side effects. There is 0.1% risk of seizures with TMS treatment. As of December 2021, SoCal TMS Center has had zero patient seizures since the practice opened.

I asked Stephanie about her personal experiences with patients receiving TMS treatment. She said that when she first meets patients they are in a "dire state". Her experience with TMS has allowed her to confidently tell patients, "You are in the right place." She does not feel ambivalent or insecure in that statement. She knows most people will respond to TMS. She is confident when she tells people it will work. As she sees them week to week, she sees the improvement in their depression. She has a front-row seat watching them change.

I have personally experienced the benefits of TMS. It has been amazing. TMS has brought a healing that I did not know existed.

It may seem odd that, as of this writing, I have done four rounds of TMS treatment. If it works, why do I keep needing to come back? That is just it. TMS does work! The times between treatments, before the depression and anxiety return, are amazing. Now I know what it is like to live without the cruel grip of depression and anxiety, even if only for months at a time.

So, I will gladly return when it is necessary. TMS makes a difference. It brings healing. TMS may not cure my mental illness, but it does enable me to experience periods when I am free of the depression and anxiety. I will gratefully welcome these times with open arms. Thank you, TMS!

13

Depression Resurfaces

Darkness Reemerges
I struggle to understand what is happening.
Everything was going so well,
But now I am tumbling.
My life is a mess again.
I cannot sleep.
Simple acts take up most of my energy.
I am surrounded by a fog.
My focus is obscured.
I do not want to do anything.
I have no motivation;
Lack the desire to be a part of anything.
Darkness rushes in once again.
I have so much to be happy about,
But I cannot enjoy it.
What is wrong with me?
Why can I not just snap out of it?
My mood drags me down.
Lack of sleep paralyzes me.
I do not want to succumb to the darkness,
But fear I will.
I have fought for so long.
The light shined briefly.
I felt so much better,
But then the darkness reemerged;
Delivered its crushing blow.
I have fallen again.
I wonder if I can ever get up.

I do not understand the waves of depression.
Will they ever remain just a ripple?
Will I ever be strong enough to surf these waves?
I thought I was doing so well.
Now I am faced with the reality that the darkness will never fade.
Darkness is always lurking;
Always haunting me.
I cannot escape the depression that grips my life.

As I was writing this section, the depression resurfaced. It had been several months since my last round of TMS. So, the downward spiral I found myself in was not really unexpected. One of the things TMS and therapy have provided me with is an understanding of my mental illness. I now better understand what I am experiencing. I can recognize when the depression is taking hold of me. I can distinguish between when the depression is caused by external factors and when it is emanating from within me. This was one of those times when I recognized that it was the illness emerging from within. As I have iterated throughout this book, depression is an illness. As with many illnesses, relapses will occur. That is how the illness works. When the relapse occurs, I need to take the necessary steps to provide myself with the treatment I need. This starts with talking to my therapist and psychiatrist. We establish that I am struggling again and that I need the treatment that works best for me. That means it is time for TMS again. I reached out to Stephanie at SoCal TMS to begin my fourth round of TMS.

It is important for individuals who live with mental illness to understand what treatment works best for them. For me it is TMS. Maybe for someone else it is ECT. Another person might respond best to hospitalization. Still others can find healing from a medication adjustment. We are all individuals and mental illness affects each of us in unique ways. Understanding what works on an individual level is instrumental to healing and recovery.

I am grateful I have a team that can assist me through this journey mental illness has taken me on throughout my life. Knowing that Dr. Sullivan, Dr. Klein, and Stephanie are actively involved in my health care make a huge difference in my ability to cope. I would even include my primary care provider, Cristina Rosales, in this group because mental health is a part of total health. Mental health care is health care.

As I waited to begin a new round of TMS treatment, I tried to remain confident that I would experience healing once again. I told myself that the darkness that reemerged would not last. TMS would help as it has each time before. Yes, it is a commitment. But taking care of all aspects of our health is a commitment. If we want to be truly healthy individuals, we must do whatever is necessary to maintain that health. For me, that means returning to TMS when the depression is in control. I have accepted this as a part of life. I am grateful for the ability to receive treatment. Too many people do not have access to the mental health care they so desperately need. That is a fact that we, as a society, must fight to change. Everyone deserves access to mental health care. It should be considered as normal as a yearly physical exam; as normal as seeing a doctor when the flu strikes. Mental health is a vital part of overall health and must be treated as such.

14

Depression at Its Worst

The Smothering Hand of Depression

The smothering hand of depression suffocates me.
I find myself gasping for breath as I search for meaning in my life.
The depression bears down upon me,
Crushing my desires and dreams.
Underneath the weight of depression, I am weak.
I hide from life.
Afraid to push back against the depression that has been a part of my life for so long.
I do not remember life without it.
As I struggle, my hope dwindles.
The hand presses down more firmly.
I cannot get back up.
The smothering hand of depression has taken my life.

For most of my life I have turned to writing when the depression gets bad. My writing has usually taken the format of poetry and journaling. Often it has allowed me to cope with the depression. I am in the midst of one of the worst downward spirals of depression that I have experienced in a long time. Dr. Sullivan suggested that I work on writing this book as a means of coping and keeping myself busy. In order to do that I need to describe what the depression is like at its worst.

Where should I start? The familiar darkness surrounds me. It is difficult to describe what I am feeling in just one sentence or even a paragraph. Actually, I am not sure I can put into words what I am truly feeling. For starters, all my thoughts are negative. They challenge everything I do; everything I say. These thoughts tell me I am worthless; that I am not lovable. After discussing it with Dr. Klein, I realized it was feelings of worthlessness that triggered this latest bout of depression. Once the feelings grabbed hold, they would not stop. I kept hearing that I was not worth anyone's time; that I did not matter. The voice in my head said I was not worth the care I needed. It became difficult to fight these thoughts off. Each day they became more consistent. Soon the self-harm thoughts started. The self-harm thoughts are scary. I started to tell myself that I deserved to be in pain. I told myself that life was not worth living. When these thoughts start, I know I need to reach out for help, even though I find myself not wanting to reach out.

I do not think I would allow myself to make an attempt to take my life, but the thoughts of hurting myself take over. They tell me that I deserve to feel the pain. They tell me that physical pain will make the mental pain stop. I know these are lies, but I find myself believing them. The person I reach out to first is always Dr. Klein. I know he will help me silence these thoughts even if only temporarily. He listens to me explain the thoughts I am having and guides me into the realization that I cannot listen to them. He reminds me that I have overcome them before and I can overcome them again.

Self-harm thoughts are painful. They usher in a sense of hopelessness. At different points in my life these thoughts have been louder than at other points. This time they grew loud. Despite knowing on a conscious level that these thoughts were lies, I struggled with them. Often, I found myself believing their message. Obviously, that is not safe for me. Depression places me in an unsafe place. It causes me to believe lies that, when I am healthy, I know are untrue.

I reach the point at which I feel overwhelmed. Work becomes too much for me. Usually, I find that when I am teaching, the students distract me, but that is not happening this time. One day while teaching, my thoughts tell me that I should not be teaching. That has rarely happened in the moment of teaching. So, it catches me off guard and I become scared. It is at this point that I recognize that I am losing in this round of depression. Still, I push through the day. I tell myself I have to keep working. My students need me to be fully present for them. Unfortunately, it is becoming apparent that I cannot be.

Just the day before, I started a new round of TMS. I told myself that if I was patient, the TMS would get me back to where I needed to be. I could still be the teacher my students needed me to be. Despite this knowledge, the voices were telling me that it was too late. Telling me that TMS would not work this time. In past rounds the TMS began to work in the third week. I told myself I could "fake it" that long. If I just gave it time, the TMS would make the depression go away.

The next morning, I went for my daily TMS treatment. Stephanie came in to talk with me. I told her how bad I was feeling. I shared how I was doubting that I could keep working. She was empathetic. I felt safe. Then the tears started. Tears just fell. It felt like my life was falling apart. I could not see the depression getting better. Stephanie understood. Her words were genuine and caring. She assured me the TMS would work again. She said she would make adjustments to try to get the effect to come on faster. We talked about whether I should be working and how I could get through this bout of the depression.

Then I drove to work. I cried the whole way. A teacher friend, Maria Perez, had to come get me from my car because I felt anxious about walking onto campus. She tried to talk me into going home, but I kept saying I had to stay. We agreed that I would get through the day and then take the next two days off. Honestly, I do not know how I got through the day. I know I was not an effective teacher that day. As soon as I got home, I left a voicemail for Dr. Klein and sent an email to Dr. Sullivan.

Everything was dark inside of me. The tears would not stop. I was shaking on the inside. I wanted everything to stop. The negative thoughts went into hyperdrive. They were ripping me apart. Telling me I was worthless. Telling me I was hurting my students. Everything seemed hopeless. I wanted to die. Dying was the only way I could see the pain ceasing.

That is the thing about depression. It is a liar. It destroys hope. Depression makes you believe that you cannot get better even when you know that is not true.

Dr. Klein called me. He helped me regain my composure a little. We talked and he told me it was okay for me to feel the way I did. He let me get out my thoughts. He reassured me. We agreed that I needed to take more than a couple days off. As we got off the phone, he told me to call him back if I needed to. I knew I had a safety net. The next day he sent me the paperwork so I could take the next four days off from work. This would allow me to rest mentally. It would also give the TMS more time to begin to take effect.

Dr. Sullivan agreed that I needed a break. I was worried about my principal finding out that I was taking this time off for my mental health. I was worried that she would not understand that depression is an illness and that I am sick. Dr. Sullivan assured me that I had a right to take this time off and that I needed it. She reminded me that the ADA laws allow me to take this time off and that my principal could not question it. The stigma exists. I was afraid to take time off for my mental health. I felt like I had to justify my illness. That is wrong. No one should have to justify taking care of their mental health.

I exchanged several emails with Dr. Sullivan on Thursday and Friday that week. I thought maybe I was bothering her. Then she said something that made me realize how lucky I am to have the mental healthcare team that I have. She told me, "I promise, you are not bothering me." I cannot even explain how much those words meant to me. In just that one sentence, Dr. Sullivan let me know I mattered. She told me that my mental health was important, and I deserved attention.

Back to what it feels like to be in the midst of depression. I feel very isolated. I feel like time has stopped. It is hard for me to do anything. Most of my time is spent lying on my bed. I just lie there. Stare at the wall or out the window. The negative thoughts swirl in my head. I feel guilty that I am not in my classroom with my students, but at the same time I know I could not be. It would not be good for me or for my students.

Each day I drive myself to TMS because despite how hopeless I feel, I know Stephanie was right. The TMS had worked before. I need to give it an opportunity to work again. I try to walk every day because it helps. Even though all I really want to do was crawl into bed and hide. I want to put a pillow over my head and muffle the thoughts that tell me I am worthless.

Thirty-five years of depression have taught me that I must fight back. Depression is vicious. It takes hold and does not want to let go. Depression hurts. The pain is beyond words. At the same time, it is numbing. Does that make sense? How can something be painful and numbing at the same time? The thoughts hurt as they swirl through my mind, but I become paralyzed. I cannot tell the thoughts to shut up. I cannot make them stop. I cannot get myself to do much of anything, which is why I usually end up in bed.

Being in bed when I am depressed is not healthy for me. It is an escape, but it does nothing to help me heal. I am not sure why I lie in bed at these times. There is a sense of safety to being under my weighted blanket. As I lie in bed the weight of my gray blanket provides a sense of touch. The weight is strangely soothing. The companies that sell these blankets likely have research to explain this. I just know I feel safer.

Another thing about depression is it steals the sense of safety from me. The self-harm thoughts that arise scare me. I have fought them off for years. It has been about 30 years since I have actually tried to end my life, but the thoughts frequently plague me. I fear that one day I may not be able to fight them off. The strange part is that I do not think it is the dying that I fear. I worry about what it would do to others. How would it be explained to my students? To my niece and nephew? I would be sending them the wrong message. Would they understand that the pain was just too much to keep hiding? Would they hate me for being too weak to keep living?

By no means am I saying that a person who dies by suicide is weak. It takes strength to live with mental illness. The concern about being viewed as weak stems from the stigma that surrounds mental health. Mental illness is so misunderstood in society. It saddens me to see it. It hurts me to experience it.

Part of the plight that most of us who live with mental illness struggle with is the stigma attached to it. As I discuss in other chapters, stigma is real. For the most part, society does not view mental illness as a true health problem. I have experienced stigma in my family, in the workplace, and in health care. It hurts. Stigma causes shame and embarrassment. Often, it increases my depression.

Stigma results from a lack of understanding. Outside of mental health professionals and people who live with mental illness, so many people lack the understanding that mental illness is a health problem. Many strides have been made to bring awareness to mental health, but we still have a long way to go to erase the stigma.

This bout of depression would prove to be difficult. I ended up taking more than a week off work, followed by spring break. I was basically away from teaching for about two weeks. I needed the time away. There was no doubt. I was grateful that I could take the time I needed. Still, I kept the reason quiet. My principal only knew I was sick. My students were told that I was not feeling well. I felt it was better that way. It gave me the time to heal without being questioned.

TMS proved effective once again. I was able to fight the depression another time. It is difficult when I am in the midst of these bouts of depression. Healing seems impossible. These times require me to trust that the light of healing will return. That is not easy. Luckily, I have a caring mental health team to assist me.

15

After TMS

TMS

At my darkest depths, when I had almost given up hope,
An opportunity was handed to me.
I was given a new chance to live;
Brought into the light of healing.
Hope once again resides inside me.
Modern technology healing my innermost being.
Technology I only vaguely understand has given me the ability to be whole;
The fortune to know that life is worth living.

Each day I recline in a chair.
Magnetic pulses tap away on my brain,
Somehow healing the brokenness,
Alleviating my depression, soothing my anxiety.

The magnetic pulses tap, tap, tap.
I wonder how it works.
It seems like magic, this machine that brings healing.
TMS, transcranial magnetic stimulation, offers a healing I can attain nowhere else.

I have entrusted my healing to their care.
Knowing TMS has worked before, hoping it will again.
They ask me how I am doing, check on me, support me through this process.
Their smiles let me know they truly care.

I am forever grateful to the team that provides this treatment.
Who, with their smiles, offer hope.
Knowing their machine holds the key to my healing,
I trust I will heal.

I have told you that TMS works, but you may wonder how I know it works. It is difficult to describe. The healing starts as a slow process.

Then suddenly I feel lighter. The sense of heaviness that accompanies the depression lifts. I feel lighter mentally. I do not feel the heavy weight of my thoughts and emotions. It is as if they have floated away, like a cloud sailing through the blue sky. As I look up, I can see that blue sky. I no longer feel tied down by mental illness. The grip of depression not only loosens; it lets go. This is an amazing feeling.

Suddenly, I realize that I am okay. I am more than okay. I experience healing. I realize that I am not internalizing everything. My thoughts do not dwell on negativity. The self-blame and constant questioning go away. My mind is freer. It can see the positive in situations. My self-talk takes on a new, more positive tone. Depression is no longer ruling my self-talk. I have regained control. I stop overthinking. I possess the power to tell negative thoughts and ideas to stop.

I am able to separate outside stressors from my emotions and feelings. Work issues no longer overwhelm me. I can maintain the separation between my job and my self-worth. I understand the difference between frustration and anxiety. I have the ability to maintain professional distance. That is something that is hard to do when the mental illness is in control. As I heal, I am better able to leave work at work.

I possess the ability to clearly communicate with others. Depression and anxiety do not get in the way. Conversations do not make me anxious. I engage in social conversations. Holding up my part of a conversation is no longer a battle. I am not withdrawn. I feel like I make meaningful contributions to conversations. My voice becomes stronger. The meek voice that depression produces is gone.

No longer frozen by the mental illness, I regain interest in doing things. I am able to do the simple things—like cook, read, watch television, create, and take care of myself—that are so difficult when the depression is pressing down upon me. This may seem like a little thing, but it is a huge achievement. Not being able to do the simple activities in life is debilitating. TMS returns my ability to not only engage in these activities but allows me to enjoy them.

Thoughts of escaping life no longer fill my mind. The self-harm thoughts dissipate. I can enjoy life. When you have lived without that enjoyment, you learn to value it. I am grateful that TMS and my mental health team have given me back that ability. Now I want to live. As someone who has struggled with suicidal ideation, the desire to live is a gift.

TMS gives me a sense of hope. As I heal, I realize there are reasons for me to be hopeful. I understand that life is worth living. This hope allows me to see that life does not have to be controlled by the darkness of depression and anxiety. Hope is a powerful tool in life. Hope makes the future worth living to be a part of.

Now when I smile, I mean it. I am not hiding behind a fake smile. I am not trying to make others believe I am okay when I am not. I am actually okay. TMS brings that realization on without warning. It just suddenly hits me. That is how I know TMS has done its job. Rather, TMS has given its gift. Healing is a gift; a present I open like a child on Christmas morning.

As I neared the end of my last round of TMS, this healing I am describing came on without warning. Maybe my brain "turned on". The circuits that needed to connect, connected. Whatever happened, however doctors explain it, I am better. I feel good. My mood is lighter. I see my life as worth living. I sense my purpose in life. I am not depressed. That was the goal. TMS made good on its promise.

I realize that not everyone will experience the same healing I have experienced. TMS brings hope. I am one example of how it has worked. I believe it can bring this healing to others. If other treatments have not worked, take a chance on TMS. Going through treatment is a commitment and it requires patience, but it is worth it. I am grateful that Dr. Sullivan and Dr. Klein encouraged me to try it. I am grateful that Dr. Hutton has made a treatment that works for me available. I am grateful that Stephanie Debnath encouraged and guided me throughout treatment. I am grateful for the nurses and techs who were by my side every day of treatment. Recovering from mental illness requires commitment and a team. We cannot travel this journey alone. Trust that there are people out there who are willing to guide you on the healing journey. Seek them out. Find what works for you. Do not give up. Healing is possible. Even in our darkest moments we must reach out. Others have to reach in as well. It is a team effort.

This is not the end of my journey. I will likely have to return for more TMS treatment at some point. That is okay. I will live to the best of my ability until then. When it is time, I will reach out. TMS will be there, and we will embark on the treatment journey again.

16

Surgery Takes Its Toll

Healing Trust

So much unknown surrounds me.
Fear consumes me.
I am anxious as I lie in a hospital bed.
Words comfort me;
Let me know I am not alone.
Doctors come in and out.
I feel overwhelmed.
Surgery looms.
Treatment after treatment awaits me.
The nurses see my anxiety;
Know I am struggling.
They reach out with a tender touch,
A reassuring word.
I am grateful for their understanding;
Relieved to not be ignored.
Assured by their presence.
I allow myself to trust
As my healing journey continues.

During the process of writing this book I had surgery. It was supposed to be a routine surgery with a fairly quick recovery. Life did not turn out as planned. The results have impacted not only my physical health, but my mental health as well.

I have always been a large-breasted woman. From an early age I was told that my figure resembled my aunt's. She died in her early 30s from breast cancer. As a result, I have had yearly mammograms for about 20 years now. My large breasts have caused other issues, including back, neck, and chest pain. Several months ago, it reached a point where I had to do something. My primary care provider, Cristina, and I discussed it. I was tired of the pain, tired of thinking about the possibility of breast cancer. Cristina referred me to a surgeon to discuss breast reduction surgery. The surgeon, Dr. Rizvi, agreed that a breast reduction was medically necessary. After a brief battle with my insurance, surgery was scheduled.

As the surgery approached, my friend, Sarah, suggested that I consider how surgery would affect my mental health. I had just finished round four of TMS. Mentally I was in a good place, but I did not want surgery to jeopardize that. I asked Dr. Rizvi if the surgery would affect my mental health. My concern was becoming depressed after surgery. He did not seem to understand my concern. He said I would be fine and asked why I was concerned. After explaining that I have a mental illness, I told him I did not want the surgery to trigger anything. I had the feeling that he did not understand my concern. He assured me there was no connection between surgery and mental health.

Not content with his answer, I consulted Dr. Sullivan, Dr. Klein, and Stephanie Debnath. They all acknowledged that a connection could be possible but were confident we could deal with any downturns in my mood. Dr. Sullivan and Dr. Klein would continue their regular appointments with me. Dr. Klein reminded me that he is always available when I am in crisis. Stephanie scheduled a follow-up appointment with me a few weeks after the scheduled surgery to check on how I was doing and evaluate if TMS would be necessary. I also talked with Cristina about the risks of the surgery. With the support of my mental health team, I felt secure in my decision to have the surgery and felt that I could handle anything it might trigger.

On the day of the surgery, I arrived at the hospital ready to undergo the operation. I was a little nervous, but I felt like I was prepared for it. Dr. Rizvi arrived in pre-op to get me ready. He took measurements and drew lines on my breasts. We talked as he worked. He assured me that this surgery was necessary and would be a success. He had a comforting tone and I felt safe. A nurse wheeled me into the operating room and before I knew it, I was waking up in post-op.

The surgery lasted about five hours. Dr. Rizvi removed nine pounds of breast tissue. The nurses settled me in a private room. It was late at night. Despite taking painkillers, I felt anxious in the hospital bed. My right hand was tingling, and I felt like I did not have control over its movement. I would later find out that the position my arm was in during surgery affected a nerve causing my carpal tunnel syndrome to flare up. It would be a few days before I could use my hand normally.

I was in the hospital for three days after the surgery. Dr. Rizvi checked on me. He said the surgery had been a success. I remained in the hospital so that the nurse could empty the drainage tubes and I could be monitored. I was released with instructions on how to continue emptying the tubes and care for the incision.

At home I was on my own. I had to take care of the tubes, which was something I had been concerned about. Fortunately, I was able to do it. Most of my time was spent in bed. Several days later I saw Dr. Rizvi in his office. He said I seemed to be healing well. His assistant removed the drainage tubes and gave me instructions on how to care for the incision and nipples. I had to bandage them and apply an antibiotic ointment daily. Once home, I followed the instructions and did my best to heal.

I was scheduled to see Dr. Rizvi again on the following Monday, but Friday night I became concerned. Not a good feeling for my mental health. There was excessive draining from the incision and nipples, especially my right nipple. I was not sure what to do, but I knew something was not right. It was after-hours so I could not call Dr. Rizvi or Cristina. So, I called my insurance company to find out what urgent care to go to. I was told the urgent care centers affiliated with my medical group were closed, but I could go to the emergency room. I was hesitant to do this. As I sat there, I could feel my depression and anxiety amping up. Negative thoughts were swirling in my mind.

Since I was not sure that this warranted an emergency room trip, I called the 24-hour nurse line on the back of my medical card. After I explained what I was experiencing, the nurse recommended that I go to the emergency room at the hospital where I had the surgery to be examined. I had not driven since before the surgery. That left me with no way to get to the hospital on my own. I took an Uber. As I sat in the back of a stranger's car, my depression and anxiety were intensifying. I was left to deal with this alone.

The emergency room was crowded. They took my vitals and told me to sit in the waiting room. A little while later the triage nurse assessed me. Again, I was sent to wait. After a while, blood was drawn and an IV line inserted. Yet again, I was sent back into the waiting room. It was late. My friends were all asleep. I had no one to text or call for comfort. Finally, I saw a doctor. She had me take my shirt off, but she did not remove the bandages that covered my incision and nipples. She made a comment about surgeons not liking other doctors to touch their work. I found this hard to believe. Surely, Dr. Rizvi would want me to be checked. The doctor sent me for an ultrasound of my right breast. She explained that they could only do one side in the ER. I did not understand why. Then I was brought back and told to sit in the waiting room again. After what seemed like forever, a nurse called me up and said I was being released. I did not see the doctor again for the results of the ultrasound or to find out what was going on. I was given a prescription for an antibiotic and told to see the surgeon on Monday. By this point it was 3:00 a.m. and I did not have the strength to question anything. I was completely on edge. My anxiety had taken over. I was convinced something bad was happening, but I was unable to do anything about it. I walked out of the emergency room and ordered an Uber.

The weekend was rough for me. I took the antibiotics and kept applying the ointment Dr. Rizvi's assistant had given me. I was scared that something was wrong. All I could do was wait for my appointment Monday afternoon. Waiting is not good for my mental health. Depression and anxiety took advantage and sent negative messages in motion in my mind.

Finally, Monday afternoon arrived. Dr. Rizvi took one look at my chest and said I needed to be readmitted to the hospital. The incision was infected, and the nipples were necrotic. He needed to do surgery again. His assistant told me to drive my car home, eat something because it would be a long night, and get a ride to the emergency room. I was going to be admitted through the emergency room. I was apprehensive about that after my recent experience there. I drove home, shaking. My friends, Maria and Gus, brought me some food, which I barely ate, and drove me to the hospital. Maria tried to stay with me, but the hospital would not allow visitors. I was on my own again.

This time I did not have to sit in the waiting room as long. I was brought back and hooked up to an IV shortly. A doctor examined me. Thankfully, it was a different doctor than Friday night. A nurse did an EKG. Then I sat hooked up to the IV in a hallway for what seemed like forever before being taken to a room.

It was late. The nurses settled me in a bed. By this point I was very anxious. The nurses were very reassuring. Soon I was asleep with no idea what was to come in the next week. I awakened several times unsure of what was going on. In the morning the nurses told me I was on a liquid diet because I would be having surgery. I did not have the surgery until Wednesday afternoon. An infection doctor came to see me. She explained that the infection needed to be cleaned out and that Dr. R would do surgery. I was on IV antibiotics. My blood pressure was high. For some reason they took me off one of my blood pressure medications. I did not understand. I did not ask questions. I became quite passive, which often happens when I am anxious.

Late Wednesday afternoon I was wheeled to pre-op. I was nervous. I did not know what another surgery would entail, and I had not spoken to Dr. Rizvi yet. It was cold in pre-op. The nurse put another blanket on me. My mind continued to swirl with anxious thoughts. Finally, Dr. Rizvi arrived. He told me everything would be fine. He would go in and clean out the infection and remove the necrotic tissue. He said he might have to operate twice. Dr. Rizvi was reassuring, and I felt safe with him. Then he disappeared to prep for the surgery. A few minutes later I was wheeled into the operating room. I do not remember anything after being moved to the surgery bed. I woke up in post-op and was quickly brought back to my room. I was grateful for that because the nurses who took care of me were all so understanding.

Dr. Rizvi checked in the next day. He explained that I was going to get hyperbaric treatment. I had never heard of hyperbaric treatment. He told me that I would be placed in a chamber so I could receive oxygen that would heal the wounds. I envisioned being plunged into a tank. Needless to say, my anxious thoughts went into overdrive. I did not know what to expect. He told me I would have one treatment before my next surgery, which was scheduled for Friday afternoon.

The nurses were great about helping me calm down. They eased my fears and helped me realize that the doctors were doing what was best for me. Being in the hospital was difficult because I felt very alone. I had no visitors, except for my brother who stopped by briefly on Sunday. There were some text messages and a phone call with Dr. Klein, but that was it. The aloneness triggered my depression. It always does. So, this was no surprise. The dialogue in my head was difficult to stop. I was dwelling on being alone and being afraid. That is what my brain does. The negative thoughts take over. I become trapped in their endless cycle. Imagine being depressed, anxious, and physically unwell at the same time. I spent most of my time sleeping or just lying in the hospital bed staring at the ceiling. My only conversations were with the nurses. I was grateful for their positiveness.

When I was wheeled down for the first hyperbaric treatment, I had no idea what to expect. The young man wheeling my bed was friendly. He made sure I was covered and masked. The first things I saw when we entered the center for treatment were two big tanks. They reminded me of submarines. Was I really going to be placed inside one of these tanks?

In the hyperbaric center I met Lili and Hector. Little did I know at that moment, these two people would get me through a lot of anxiety and make treatment easier for me. Right away they explained what I would be experiencing. I think they sensed my fear. They took their time with me and were very understanding. When it was time for me to enter the tank, they did it slowly, making sure I was comfortable. In the beginning I thought I would only get a few of these treatments. I would end up having over 30 treatments. Lili and Hector were by my side the whole time.

The hyperbaric chamber is a tube. It is just longer than an average person's height. It fits a bed that is wheeled on a track into it. There is not much room to move. Not that there is much need to move. It feels tight in there. The windows resemble the circular windows on a submarine. There are windows to each side of where my head rested. On one side I could see Hector or Lili and talk to them through a microphone. The other side had a television screen outside of it. It was on this screen that I watched many movies over the course of treatment.

This first time was scary. Hector asked if I would like him to say a prayer before he pushed me into the tube. I gratefully said yes. Oddly, it eased my anxiety a bit. Hector or Lili said a prayer before every session. The prayers made me feel comfortable.

Hyperbaric treatment is hard on the ears. There is a change in pressure, which is similar to being in an airplane. I had to learn how to get my ears to pop. In the beginning this was a problem for me and made the treatment uncomfortable.

After the first treatment I was wheeled back to my room. The nurse eagerly asked questions about the treatment. It felt good to discuss what I had just been through. My blood pressure was still high, and I was concerned. I did not understand why they had taken me off the blood pressure medication. The nurse said there was something in my chart about my potassium level being high. She thought that might be connected to why they took me off the medication. A doctor specializing in the kidneys came in to see me. I was confused. What could be wrong with my kidneys? He said very little. I was not in the frame of mind to ask questions. The nurse explained that the amount of antibiotics I was on might be affecting my kidneys. I would see three different kidney doctors while I was in the hospital. None of them really explained anything. One of them ordered an ultrasound on my kidneys. I was later told the results were okay. No one ever explained what they were looking for, which increased my anxiousness.

As I was in the hospital and not understanding things with my blood pressure and kidneys, I found myself wishing my primary, Cristina, was the one taking care of me. At least she would explain things. It is funny. I trust a physician's assistant more than doctors. I guess that is because she takes more time to ensure that I understand what is going on and she understands my mental illness causes me to have extra needs.

The nurses seemed to understand that, too. I think it was Thursday night that I had a bad anxiety attack in the middle of the night. I was lying in the dark and just could not get my thoughts to stop. I felt shaky. The nursing assistant helped me to the restroom. While in there I started to dry heave. I did not understand what was going on. This was a bad anxiety attack. I wanted to scream for it to stop. The nursing assistant called the nurse. She came and sat with me. She did not do anything special. She just talked to me. She asked me about my anxiety. She told me she understood. She shared that she sometimes feels anxious. It helped. After a while I was able to get back into bed and relax. The nurse cared enough to make sure my mental health was tended to, not just my physical health. I really appreciated that.

Surgery number three took place Friday evening. As with the first two surgeries, Dr. Rizvi saw me beforehand. He reassured me again. His smile and tone were comforting. I was a little more prepared for the third surgery because I had learned what to expect. This would be more cleaning out of infection and necrotic tissue. Again, it was over before I knew it.

Monday and Tuesday I had more hyperbaric treatment. Lili and Hector helped me through it. Each treatment lasted two hours. That is a long time to be stuck in a tube. They would pick movies for me to watch. I was too anxious to pick a movie from their list myself. It was just too overwhelming. They checked on me frequently, coming to the window to see how I was doing. That helped a lot. It made me feel less alone and eased my anxiety a little.

Tuesday night I was finally released from the hospital. I had been there for eight days. Dr. Rizvi removed the drainage tubes. I was glad to not have to care for those at home. I was nervous about the infection coming back. He promised me I was going to be okay. Two antibiotics were prescribed to replace the IV antibiotics I had been on. My friend, Carol, picked me up and got me settled in at home.

For the next month or so I would have daily treatment at the hyperbaric center. Lili and Hector took great care of me. They comforted me when I needed comforting. They eased my anxiety when I was anxious. Getting in the tube provoked my anxiety. Dr. Sullivan prescribed a low dose of medication to help me with the anxiety. Lili and Hector were understanding and made it easier for me. I am grateful for their empathy and care.

As of this writing, I am still healing. It has been a long process. I learned a lot about the connection between my physical and mental health. They definitely affect each other. As I struggled with the infection and the effects of surgery, my depression and anxiety were triggered. I had to deal with the negative thoughts that swirl in my mind when the mental illness is in control. I had to learn to cope with my anxiety so that I could receive hyperbaric treatment. I had to trust healthcare providers. I learned that I could trust them. Dr. Rizvi, the nurses, Lili, and Hector showed me that they cared enough to understand how my mental health was affected by what I was going through physically. This gives me hope for health care. I have had negative experiences with healthcare providers in the past. I am grateful that this experience was different.

17
How "Let It Go" Saved My Life

Grace

A soulful voice serenades me as I contemplate life.
Raw emotion overpowers my pain.
The voice soothes me; settles my anxiety.
Lyrics written as if intended for me.
I feel the energy; engage in healing.
Songs speaking directly to me.
When I am about to break, I turn to the voice.
It lifts me from the brink as it always has.
The voice has taught me to "Let It Go" and hold onto life.
I close my eyes; allow the voice to carry me into the lyrics and away from life.

As a teenager there were many times when I just did not want to live. My mind was overrun with what I now know was suicidal ideation. I wrote poetry about dying. I thought about it constantly. Now, secure in a locked briefcase, I have the journals, red spiral notebooks, I wrote poetry in during that time. Fear of what those journals contain has prevented me from rereading them. Could reading these words trigger painful thoughts? I know they are filled with poems in which I either expressed a desire to die or actually "died" in the poem.

It was around that same time that I discovered alcohol. When I was drinking, the pain would subside or at least it felt like it did. Many mornings I woke up not knowing how I ended up in my bed.

I kept a knife in my bedroom. It was a kitchen knife with a dark brown, wooden handle. Thoughts of slitting my wrist became obsessive. I would rub the knife against the pale skin of my left wrist. Little red scratches would appear. Sometimes I would draw a few tiny drops of blood. It was difficult to understand, but this felt good. I did not understand why I was cutting myself. What I really wanted to do was shut out the darkness. I just wanted the dark feelings to go away. I remember telling myself that death had to be better. Now that I have an understanding of self-harming behaviors, I realize that I was cutting.

At these times I always listened to music. Jefferson Airplane was my favorite band. I discovered a solo album by Grace Slick, one of their lead singers. The album, Dreams, was from 1979. There were two songs on this album, "Let It Go" and "Do It the Hard Way", that really resonated with me. I would play them over and over, knowing exactly where to place the needle on the black vinyl. It was as if Grace Slick was singing directly to me. Somehow the music filled me and comforted me.

I distinctly remember drinking and holding a knife to my wrist, ready to end my life, while listening to the album. The knife's sharp edge grazing my skin leaving scratches. My body shaking. My face streaked with tears. Then I would hear Grace Slick singing, "Let It Go". Slowly I would let the knife go and watch it fall onto the carpet in front of my stereo. Somehow, Grace's singing got me to drop the knife each time.

Does music really have that power? Can the words of a songwriter bring a person back from the brink of self-harm and suicidal thoughts? I can only speak from my own experience. Yes, music has that power. The singer/song-writer can connect with the listener. I honestly believe that through her songs, Grace Slick stopped me from taking my own life. I played the song repeatedly. It gave me a sense that someone cared. Grace was there for me when no one else was. I still play "Let It Go" when I am struggling. Grace's voice comforts me even now 30-plus years later.

In 2019, I had the opportunity to meet Grace Slick. Even though it had been over 30 years since her music saved my life, the memory remains with me. Grace Slick, now an artist, was showing her art at a gallery in Holly-wood. Of course, I had to get tickets. My friend, Carol Nichols, drove me there. I was too nervous to drive.

It was a small gallery, but it was packed. I walked around looking at the paintings, feeling nervous. Slick's talent was apparent in every painting. Any minute Grace Slick would be walking in. Could I get myself to talk to her? I wanted to thank her. Without her music, it is possible I would not have lived past my teen years.

When she walked in, I felt myself shaking. She sat down and a line immediately formed. I tentatively joined the line. In my head I went over what I wanted to say. I was afraid it would not come out right. I feared that I would not be able to express just how much her music has meant in my life and the power her words contained.

I reached the front of the line. She looked amazing. I was in awe. Here I was standing in front of the woman who in my time of deep darkness told me to "Let It Go". I opened my mouth. Somehow the words came out. I told her how much her song "Let It Go" meant to me. She made a joke about how she should have gotten money from the Frozen version of the song. I told her that her song saved my life. I shared how when I wanted to kill myself, her words stopped me.

Grace Slick looked at me intently. She smiled and said, "No, you did that. You were the strong one."

It was so powerful to be told that I was strong by someone I idolized. I pulled my third book, Curative Quest: Mental Health, Hope, and Healing, out of my purse. I had written a poem about her impact. The poem is simply titled, "Grace". Handing her the book, I told her that I wanted her to have it as a thank-you for what she had done for me. She took the book and thanked me. I had to step aside at that point because the line was growing impatient behind me.

Music is powerful. The lyrics to "Let It Go", written for another purpose, saved my life. Obviously, Grace Slick did not intend to save my life with her words. She had her own reasons for writing and singing the song. But her words found me, spoke to me. Call it fate or just dumb luck, but "Let It Go" stopped me from making an attempt on my life. The fact that I can still find comfort in it today speaks to the power of the words. We never know the effect our words will have on others. Whether in song, book, or conversation, words have power. Grace Slick's words spoke to me and gave me the courage to "Let It Go".

18

Music's Gift

Music Heals

Symphonic voices fill the air.
I gently sway to the music.
A sense of calm washes over me.
Peace enters my mind as the lyrics replace the noise.
Rhythmic beating, energizing riffs soothe me.
The anxiety within me abates.
I become one with the music;
Lose myself as the song takes over.
The chorus repeats.
I listen to its message and understand.
My body relaxes as the tension leaves me.
The music frees me; allows me to heal.

Sometimes when I am depressed, anxious, or both, I turn to music. Usually, my intent is for it to be a distraction. Instead, it often provides a much-needed salve. It is hard to know what is happening, but the right music can be soothing. Oftentimes it can lift the anxiety off me or lighten the darkness of my depression. I have already explained the immense power of Grace Slick's lyrics in my life. There is other music, too.

When the depression and anxiety take over, sometimes my favorite music can be soothing. Generally, the music I choose would not be classified as soothing. My preference is rock music, specifically the music of the band Styx. There is something in the guitar riffs, the beat of the drums, the melody of the keyboards that reaches me in a way nothing else can. The voices of Tommy Shaw, James Young, and Lawrence Gowan sing straight to me. I become lost in their music.

Often, the depression or anxiety have me in tears or "trapped" in my bed when I turn to their music. I hear Tommy singing "Crystal Ball", my personal favorite, and I escape into the lyrics. As I write this paragraph, I hear the words and I feel as if I could reach out and touch that crystal ball. I feel connected to someone. That connection to another person is something I so often lack. Maybe that is what the music does for me. It connects me to a group of guys whose music is a healing gift.

Friends tease me because I have been to so many Styx concerts. Forty, at last count. Most of the time I go to Styx concerts by myself. After all, I can only ask the same people to go so many times. Usually, crowds make me more anxious. When Styx is playing, that anxiety disappears. It is like I have escaped into another world. I feel safe. There is a lifting of the darkness, even if it is only for the couple hours of the concert. My usually rigid body loosens. I sway to the music. A smile emerges on my face.

Thank you, Tommy, JY, Lawrence, Todd, Ricky, and Chuckie.

What is it about music that releases this healing salve? I do not understand how it happens. I just know music heals me at times. Music is the friend, the family, that I so often feel I am lacking.

In 2016, I was having a rough summer. I had attended a Styx concert locally. While it helped, it just was not enough. My friend, Carol Nichols, suggested that I go to another concert. As luck would have it, they were playing north of here in a few days. Carol convinced me to buy a ticket and get a hotel room because it was a little far to drive back from afterward. I drove north to Ventura County. My hotel was right on the beach. I arrived too early to check in to the hotel, so I was hanging around outside the front doors gazing at the beach. I was out there for a while when walking toward me I saw someone who looked familiar. As he neared, I realized it was Lawrence Gowan, keyboardist and vocalist for Styx. I could not have planned it any better because I was wearing a Lawrence Gowan t-shirt. He walked up to me and started talking. Lawrence Gowan, a man whose music had calmed me so many times, was talking to me. He said he loved my t-shirt. Then he took my cell phone, put his arm around me, and took our picture. Now enlarged to an 8x10, that picture is hanging on my living room wall. He said goodbye and walked into the hotel. I could not believe it. I was staying in the same hotel as Styx.

After that I could not leave the area. I found a seat in the lobby. A short time later James Young (JY) came down. I smiled. He stopped to talk to me. I told him how much I loved his music and that it always helped me through difficult times. I told him I had come up for the concert because I could not get my anxiety to go away and was hoping a night of Styx music would help. He jokingly told me that I needed to smoke a joint. Then he took a picture with me. That framed 8x10 is also on my living room wall.

A few minutes later Tommy Shaw walked through the lobby. I asked him if he was going to sing "Crystal Ball" that night. He said he would. Then he took a picture with me, which is the third picture adorning my living room wall.

It was a great concert that night. A security guard gave me a pass to get closer. It was a magical night. Carol was right. I needed to go up to Ventura to see Styx. By spending a few minutes of their time with me, three of my favorite musicians proved that music is healing and that musicians have a special connection to their fans. Meeting Lawrence, JY, and Tommy was healing and provided my greatest Styx memory.

One of the pluses of modern technology is having our favorite music in one place. I made a playlist on my iPhone of the songs that soothe me. These songs help me when the depression and anxiety become difficult to cope with. Of course, Grace Slick's "Let It Go" is on this playlist. I have included several Styx songs. Some songs the guys have performed as solo acts are on the playlist. REO Speedwagon, Stevie Nicks, and Jefferson Airplane all make appearances. When I am struggling, one of my coping strategies involves listening to this playlist. After a few songs I feel myself calming a bit. I try to focus my mind on the lyrics to distract myself from the thoughts that my mental illness thinks I should be paying attention to. This helps. The music serves as a calming distraction. It does not make the depression and anxiety go away, but it helps me cope better. That is music's power. I sometimes wonder if these musicians know the power of their music. Theirs is a healing gift.

19

The Importance of Family and Friends

A Friend

A friend sits next to me.
It comforts me to know she is there.
Words do not have to be exchanged.
Presence is powerful.
Just knowing she is there eases my anxiety;
Enables me to relax.
So much is going on around us.
The outer world is in turmoil,
But for a brief time there is calm just knowing she is here.
We must face the challenges that everyone is facing;
Confront the fear that is mounting.
With my friend by my side, I am a little less afraid.
Knowing I am not alone strengthens me; gives me hope.
We can face the world together.
We are not in this alone.
With my friend by my side, I rise up.
I am ready to be strong.

Having a loved one with a mental illness is not easy. I know it cannot be easy for my family and friends. I often isolate when I am depressed. It is difficult for me to interact. I become easily upset when I am anxious. For most of my life I have attempted to keep the depression and anxiety hidden. I have not wanted others to know. I have not wanted to bother family and friends with my mental illness.

With family, I have held back because I believed they would not understand. How do you explain to a parent why you seem so unhappy? How do you explain that you are still single because bringing another person into the world of my mental illness just seems unfair? Or that I am childless because even though I wanted to be a mother, I was afraid of passing this illness on?

These are difficult questions; questions I still do not have answers to.

Sadly, these concerns also have led to me missing out on a lot in life. Sometimes I wonder what my life would have been like if the depression had never reared its ugly head. What different choices would I have made? What experiences would I have had? I will never know.

My parents and younger brother did not know I was depressed in high school or that it continued into my adult life. I hid the depression. I did not know how to talk about it. The always-smiling high school counselor never informed my parents that I was having a problem. They probably should have been informed, but it just did not happen. So, they never knew.

After I graduated from college, I told my parents about the depression and anxiety because I was no longer able to get my medication at the university health center and I did not have medical insurance at the time. I needed financial help to get the medication. My parents were the only ones I could turn to. They were against me taking medication for mental illness. They told me I just needed to choose to be happy. I remember them buying me some makeup and a book about positive thinking. It was a well-intended effort, but not what I needed. Unfortunately, I had no way to get my medication and I had temporarily moved back to Southern California, which meant I did not have my therapist, either. I took the medication I had left until it ran out.

Toward the end of that summer, my father and I headed to Illinois in my little, red, Suzuki hatchback. I would be attending Western Illinois University as a graduate student. I had earned a position as a graduate assistant and would be working on a master's degree. We were somewhere in Texas when I became very dizzy, and we stopped at an emergency room. The doctor told me it was withdrawal symptoms from going off my medication, but I could not tell my dad that. I do not remember if I came up with the story myself, or if a doctor helped, but I told my dad it was an ear infection. We picked up a prescription, which he thought was an antibiotic, but was really an antidepressant. The next day we made it to the small university town in Illinois. My dad dropped me off and left, unaware that I was back on antidepressants.

Part of settling into my new home required finding a doctor to prescribe medication for my depression and anxiety. I also needed a therapist. It was a small town, but I jumped on both tasks. I had a university health center to rely on again. My year of graduate school was uneventful. I took my medicine and went to therapy. I earned a master's degree. The greatest lesson I learned was to keep my mental illness to myself. I did not bring it up with family again until I was in my forties and had accepted my mental illness.

A few years ago, through my acceptance of having a mental illness, I learned that I had a great-aunt who struggled with her own depression at times. It was comforting to have her support and understanding. She and my cousin are still the only family members who have been to one of my speaking engagements. I appreciate the support. Maybe one day my mom will make it to one of my talks or book releases. If not, it is okay. I understand. I am sure is difficult to understand what I have struggled with as a result of mental illness. Knowing that she cannot ease my pain must be difficult. I hold out hope that one day, when she is ready, she will be there to hear me share my story. My mom has purchased all my books. My guess is that my books are not easy to read for a mother, but she has made an effort.

Friends have been a lifeline for me, especially in recent years as I have found acceptance of my mental illness. They have learned about depression and anxiety and come to understand my mental illness in a way that allows them to be part of a support system for me. I have three close friends who are not only aware of my depression and anxiety, but also very aware of my coping skills. Having friends who know my coping skills and are willing to remind me to engage in these skills is a blessing. Sometimes Sarah, Shannon, and Carol notice that I am spiraling down before I am willing to recognize it. They might ask something as simple as, "Are you okay?" Or they might remind me that I should try one of my coping skills. Many times, they have suggested I put on some music. Actually, it is more like, "Why don't you blast some Styx?"

Other times just having my friends by my side is enough. Nothing needs to be said or done. Just being there provides me with a sense of safety and allows me to know someone cares. We do not need to discuss what my depression or an anxiety are doing. It is enough just to have someone by my side. Maybe they are distracting me from the effects of my illness. Maybe my friends are creating another reality to counter the power of the depression and anxiety. I am not sure what is happening. The thing I do know is that having friends who are supportive and willing to be there makes a difference.

Until recently I did not realize how much my mental illness affects my friends. I spiraled far down during my most recent bout with depression. When I am going through these times it is difficult to be aware of how others are reacting to it. I was having self-harm thoughts, but I had never shared those particular thoughts with my friend, Carol Nichols. It was something I had never wanted to burden her with as a friend. As the TMS was bringing me out of the bout of depression, Carol mentioned that she had been worried I would hurt myself. I did not realize that she knew my mind went to self-harm thoughts. I had never said anything about those thoughts to her. It hurt to know that I had worried my friend. I explained that my mind does go there, but that when it happens, I know to alert my mental health team. The thoughts are hard to fight, but I know I can battle with the right help.

This discussion with Carol made me realize she was more in tune with me than I had thought. As a result, I vowed to be more honest. I do not have to try to protect her by not saying anything when the self-harm thoughts are present. She is aware and is going to be worried whether I say anything or not. For this reason, it is better to be open. If I am honest about what I am feeling and thinking, then I can also be honest about the help I am receiving. Honesty is better for my friends and family.

Over the years I have avoided relationships. I have not been on a date in over 20 years. The reason seems rational to me. I do not want to bring another person into my struggle with mental illness. It does not seem fair. I have often questioned who could love a person so shrouded in darkness. I have wondered if I am capable of loving another person when I do not love myself. It has come up in therapy many times. Dr. Klein has encouraged me to take risks in this area. Friends have tried to get me to try online dating sites. I have just never been able to do it. Maybe as TMS and my mental health team help me find healing, that will change. I am hopeful that I will not spend the rest of my life alone. Part of me wants to know what it is like to be in a romantic relationship. I have missed out. Sometimes I feel sorry for myself because of that. Other times I accept it as just a part of my life. It is an aspect of the journey I am on.

It is too late for me to have children of my own. I no longer need to think about the possibility of passing on my mental illness to a child. As much as I think I would have liked being a mother, I could not take that risk. The fact that I could not get myself to date ensured that risk was not an issue. It is interesting that on the surface, mental illness would not seem to affect a decision to have a child. However, for me it played a huge role. My life has been difficult because of mental illness. How could I be responsible for bringing that same difficulty to someone else's life? I made my choices. I cannot go back and do it over. I will never know what it is like to be called "Mom" because of mental illness.

As I have accepted my mental illness, I have realized that I do not need to hide it from family and friends. If I treat my mental illness with the honesty I would treat a physical illness, they will see that mental illness is just that, an illness. I had to accept my mental illness before I could ask family and friends to accept it. Acceptance is critical to healing. As a sufferer I must acknowledge that my mental illness is a legitimate illness. It is as real as diabetes or cancer. Mental illness requires similar treatment approaches. If a doctor diagnosed me with cancer, I would have to accept it. The same is true for mental illness. Most people would not hide a cancer diagnosis. The same should be true for mental illness. When we battle an illness, we need support. That support comes from not only medical professionals, but also from our family and friends.

Our loved ones are an integral part of the healing process. They need an understanding of our illness and our treatment. Mental illness is not an illness that can be battled alone. It requires a team effort. It took me too long to figure that out. I am glad I finally did.

20
The Power of Writing

My Pen

When my mind is full of turmoil, I turn to my pen,
Reach for my journal and begin to write.
Words take the form of lines.
The poison pours out of me.
My pen is an instrument of healing.
The ink gives life to the words I cannot voice.
Line after line, page after page filled with my thoughts.
I feel each thought as it leaves my mind to make its mark upon the paper.
The page soaks up memories;
Becomes stained by pain.
Dark thought after dark thought is released
And allowed to breathe on the page.
In these moments, I feel lighter.
A sense of healing envelops me
As my turmoil escapes.
My pen provides this passage to healing.
Each poem I write gives me the courage to continue.
My journals hold the reality of my pain;
Relieving me of my pain
And allowing me to live.

Writing has been an instrumental facet of my healing from the beginning of my journey with mental illness. In the early days I wrote poems in red spiral notebooks, releasing the pain of my depression without understanding what I was doing. I continued to write for years. Many of those poems have been lost to misplaced journals. Others are locked up, too intense to be reread.

Dr. Klein was the first person I really shared my writing with. He saw the therapeutic value in my poetry and urged me to continue writing. With his encouragement I have taken my writing beyond just being healing for myself. I have learned to share it with others. The four poetry books I have published are a direct result of Dr. Klein's support and belief that writing is healing for me.

How does the healing take place? I am not sure I fully understand it, but I know writing is healing for me. There is a power in writing for me. I can feel the healing taking place. Thoughts swirl in my head. These thoughts travel from my head, down my arm, and into my pen. From there the words escape onto the lined pages of my journal. Once my mind is free of the thoughts, I can process the words. I can better understand what I feel. It is like I am bleeding the poison of depression and anxiety onto the page. The illness emerges from inside of me. I can see it on the pages, read it in the words. The poems that surface paint a picture of the havoc mental illness has wreaked upon me.

I think it is healthy to see the words on the page this way. I can look at them with a sense of distance. I can share them with Dr. Klein. We discuss them, figure out what they are trying to say to me. Sometimes I have difficulty voicing what I am experiencing. I feel like the depression and anxiety are trapping the pain they cause within me. At these times I struggle to tell even Dr. Klein what I am thinking. But in poetry the words escape. There is a flow to their escape.

Writing is a form of communication. My mental illness has chosen to use writing to communicate. Maybe you have to experience it to understand, but I truly believe my poetry, and sometimes my journal writing, is my mental illness talking to me. The writing is allowing me to understand what is going on in my mind. It is making sense of the swirling thoughts, giving them some sense of order. On the paper the words are more concrete. I can make sense of them when I see them in print as opposed to just hearing their racket in my brain.

I believe I have a story to tell. Everybody has a story. My story is the story of a journey. It is a long story, one filled with more downs than ups. A story filled with emotional pains and trials that have required a strength I did not realize I possessed. After all, I have fought the illness for years. My poetry tells that story. It is not a linear story, but it is filled with plot and mystery. I write about the trials my mental illness forces me to face. I write about the side trips into healing. New trials await. Much like Odysseus taking on challenges throughout The Odyssey, I take on the mental illness. I battle it when others might have fled. Just when Odysseus thinks he has defeated one monster, another one emerges. That is also true of my mental illness.

My poetry is my transcription of my journey, but it is also an instrumental part of the journey. Writing soothes me. As I mentioned earlier, I feel the poison flowing out of me as it emerges through my pen. There is healing in the release of the pain I feel. As I describe the depression in a poem, I am freeing myself of a bit of its power. That feels good. My writing extinguishes some of the depression's power. It may never fully go away. There are days when the depression will be stronger, but writing gives me a coping skill. Writing enables me to make sense out of my mental illness.

Sharing my poetry has been healing. It has allowed me to connect with others. I started with a poetry reading at a coffee house. After learning that I had been writing poetry, my friend, Sarah, talked me into sharing a few poems at a poetry reading. I was shocked when I received a good response. That, paired with Dr. Klein's encouragement, led to me publishing my first book. From there I did more poetry readings at local independent bookstores. I published a second book and continued with the poetry readings. A monthly poetry circle at an independent bookstore became my favorite outing.

A change happened when I was preparing to write my third book. I had the painful experience with my primary care provider. As I mentioned earlier, it changed my perspective on why I was writing. The poetry readings were not enough. I wanted my writing to have an impact. I started looking for organizations where I could read my poetry and give talks about mental health. My third book, Curative Quest: Mental Health, Hope, and Healing, focused on mental health. It was my entrance into mental health advocacy. With this book I was able to schedule speaking events with groups like National Alliance on Mental Illness (NAMI).

When I speak, I share my poetry. Poems are interspersed throughout the talk. People tell me they relate to my poems. They connect to how I explain my depression and anxiety. This connection helps me. It lets me know I am not alone. The connection does the same for others. As we relate to our experiences, there is a sense of healing in not being alone.

Helping others is a good feeling. It keeps me writing and sharing. One of my favorite groups to speak to is family members of individuals with mental illness. NAMI has given me that opportunity. I have found that these family members want to understand what their loved one is going through. They are hungry for that understanding. My poetry gives them an insight into what it is like to live with mental illness. No two individuals experience mental illness the exact same way, but there are similarities. When I share my experiences, I am giving family members a glimpse of what their loved one might be going through. I never realized my writing could provide such a meaningful service. In that way, my suffering has served a purpose.

Another rewarding experience my writing has provided me with is speaking to groups of individuals who, just like me, have mental illness. When I speak to these groups, I share my story of living with mental illness and include several of my poems. People connect to my poems. They tell me, "That's just how I feel," and, "Your experience is the same as mine," and, "Depression makes me feel that way, too." It is my desire to give these individuals hope. Let them see that there is a light of healing out there. The dark times of mental illness will always pop up, but the light of healing can also exist. Writing has given me that experience. Sharing my story has enabled me to grow stronger, to heal a bit more.

Writing will always be a part of my life. It is a healing tool. Really, it is a gift. I have been able to better understand my mental health because of my writing. Others have related to my writing and gained an understanding that they are not alone. Family members have gained an understanding of their loved ones. I do not know where I would be if writing were not a part of my life. I am grateful for writing's healing touch in my life.

21

Advocacy

Beacon in the Darkness

Too many of us are silenced by mental illness.
The time has come to raise our voices.
Share, advocate, and fight back.
I have a voice I must use.
So much of what I have been through has plagued others, too.
Not every one of us can speak up,
But I can share my story.
Allow my experiences to inform others.
Gain understanding for those of us who suffer.
Advocate for better treatment.
My words can make a difference.
Joined with others, we can be a force.
Those of us with mental illness deserve to be heard.
We have stories worth sharing.
So, I will use my voice;
Be a beacon in the darkness.

The shift from poet to mental health advocate was a natural one for me. I found my voice through poetry readings. It was poetry readings at Sandpiper Books and the former Pipe & Thimble Bookstore that allowed me to develop the ability to share my work with others and to be comfortable in front of an audience. The owners of these stores, Tish, Barb, and Ellie, gave me a place to develop as a speaker. After a while it was time for me to shift my focus from the poetry itself to the reason behind the poetry, mental health.

My poetry has always been about my mental health, but I came to the realization that mental health had to be the focus of my work. It was not about writing a best seller or publishing books. My work was about the message behind my words. Incidents such as being called a liability by a primary care provider because of my mental illness encouraged me to use my voice. I began searching for avenues to speak about mental health. I stumbled upon NAMI, the National Alliance on Mental Illness. One of their chapters gave me an opportunity to speak. It was a gathering of about 30 chapter members. The group listened to me with rapt attention. They asked questions. They seemed to relate to the poems I shared. Some people even bought my books. I am not good at the selling part. I am more apt to give my books away. So, my good friend and cover artist, Shannon Feldmann, came to handle that aspect of the talk. My books sold well.

Not long after this event, I was contacted by the Orange County (CA) chapter of NAMI. I spoke at a Knowledge Forum for them at a local hospital. My determination to be a mental health advocate took off. One of their coordinators encouraged me to become more involved with their chapter. I was trained as an In Our Own Voice speaker for NAMI. I have given talks in that role many times. Because of the pandemic, most of those talks have been on Zoom, which provides a simple avenue for getting my message out.

One of my favorite talks to give is through their Family-to-Family program. I get the opportunity to share my story and my poetry to family members who are learning to help their loved ones who have mental illness. These talks are powerful for me. The family members are always so interested and grateful when I speak. I gain from this experience, too. I am able to use my story to help others. It gives my journey a purpose.

I have also had the opportunity to speak to groups of people who have mental illness. One of the greatest feelings I have experienced is when someone with a mental illness connects to my poetry. My poems express my experiences with depression and anxiety. When others relate to my words, we both gain a sense of understanding. We connect on a level that is unique to individuals with mental illness and we come to understand that we are not alone. We are all searching for a connectedness, whether we are aware of it or not. Mental illness is a lonely illness. So much of what we experience is not understood by others. The ability to connect through my words is healing.

I still give talks for NAMI, but I also give talks independently. When I speak, I intersperse poems throughout my talks to give the audience a sense of what living with mental illness is like. This approach has been very successful. Each time I speak, I become more confident in my ability to use my voice.

At first, I thought I could only speak when I was feeling at my best. Dr. Sullivan helped me realize that it was not necessary for me to be feeling good to share my story. Recently, I was scheduled to give a talk to a group of people with mental illness and their therapists. I was worried because I had been struggling with my depression. I was not sure I was up to it. Dr. Sullivan encouraged me to still try and not cancel. She told me this was a group of people who would understand if I was struggling. Her words made sense and I gave the talk. I was honest when I spoke to the group. I told them I was not at my best, but that I wanted to be there. They seemed to really appreciate that. They were able to relate to what I was going through, and it turned out to be one of my best talks.

One of the group's therapists asked me if it was helpful for me to tell my story even though I was struggling. I realized that it was. In an email, I told Stephanie Debnath about this. She reminded me that people need to see all parts of the healing journey. Her words brought on a powerful awareness for me. It is okay for me to speak when I am not at my best. It is honest. Even though I am an advocate, I still struggle with my mental health. People benefit from seeing that I struggle. Mental illness is a journey. There is no shut-off valve that stops the illness. That is okay. As an individual with mental illness, I do my best to use my journey as an example. People need to see all aspects of the journey, not just the good parts. Being honest about the ups and downs of mental illness is the only way I am going to help others understand what it is like to live with mental illness.

I have a story to tell. It is a story filled with ups and downs, of pain and healing. I have had support along the way. It is now my turn to support others. I hope my advocacy work makes a difference for others. That is the reason I wrote this book. I want my story to encourage others. I want to give hope to people who have suffered. Every person who finds hope within this book gives my suffering purpose.

Even as I struggle with my own depression, I will continue to be vocal about mental health care. My experiences have led me to advocacy. I cannot be silent. I have a voice that I can use to help others who struggle. I have the means to advocate for mental health care and awareness. I must use this means and continue to advocate.

That primary care physician's assistant who called me a liability awakened a voice within me. Even though it was not her intention, she gave me a reason to advocate. Her words allowed me to understand that a stigma exists in health care. Too many healthcare providers do not understand mental health. Too many hurt the patients they are supposed to heal. She called me a liability because of my mental illness, but she is the liability. She, and the many others in her profession who uphold that stigma, are the reason there is a lack of health care for people suffering from mental illness. It is people like her that I promise to use my voice to change. I will likely never be able to address her, but I can address her peers. I can be a voice for change, a voice calling out to end the stigma.

I know there are caring healthcare providers out there. The ones who understand that mental health is important. They understand that they must address their patients' mental well-being. Some have provided me with care and made me feel safe. I thank Cristina, Greta, and M for always understanding. Now we must reach their colleagues. If I can be a part of the solution, my mental illness will have served a purpose.

Mental health advocacy is something I plan to devote more time to in the coming years. I work full time as a teacher, which makes it difficult to spend as much time advocating as I would like. I make as much time for it as I can. The emergence of Zoom presentations has provided me with more opportunities. Although, I do prefer in-person events. I wrote this book as a means of advocating, of getting the message out that people can live meaningful lives with mental illness. It is my goal to continue advocating until the stigma surrounding mental illness is erased.

22

The Big Bang Theory

Fictional Comfort

Fictional characters on a television screen comfort me;
Bring me laughter at the end of a tough day.
I find pleasure in their antics.
Safety in watching a television show I have seen many times.
The characters become my friends,
Filling a real-life void.
These characters do not see my darkness.
They just accept me for who I am.
For thirty-minute blocks I am a part of their world
And they mine.
I find companionship as I watch.
I know every scene, can recite the dialogue.
Still, I watch.
I am safe here in front of my television screen.
I laugh with these characters;
Smile as I feel a part of their friendship.
This is my nightly routine.
Engaged with fictional characters on a television screen,
I do not feel quite so alone.
My fictional friends comfort me.

There is something about routine and repetition that is soothing for me. Knowing what is going to happen calms me. Whether it is following my daily routine or watching the same television show, I find comfort in routine. Television watching is where this is most noticeable. I think it has to do with more than just comfort, though. I have also found a sense of companionship in watching the same television show.

So, what show do I watch? The Big Bang Theory. I have seen every episode multiple times, yet I watch it almost every evening. The characters have become my nightly "friends". Yeah, I get that that sounds strange, but it is the feeling I get. I feel comfortable watching them even if I know the next line before it is spoken. I feel safe. There will be no surprises, no anxiety-producing twists. Just a group of people who I have become accustomed to "hanging out" with.

I am not sure how this started. Thanks to syndication, I am able to watch my "friends" almost nightly. Often, I am not even fully paying attention. But I can look up at any moment and fit right into the situation. For me that is a comforting feeling. The characters in this show are a group of friends. Even though I have friends, I do not have the close relationships this group of individuals has developed. Maybe I have been longing for the type of friendship they have. Maybe it would make me less alone and in doing so alleviate some of the depression. That is a lot of pressure to place on fictional characters. Shannon refers to The Big Bang Theory as my friends. Sometimes I will get a text from Shannon asking if I am watching my friends. I wonder if she thinks I am weird for having fictional friends. It does not really matter what anyone else thinks. At least I am not completely alone when I am watching.

I have read that people with mental health disorders, particularly anxiety, tend to have a show or two that they watch frequently, no matter how many times they have seen it. I guess I should be counted in that group. I do not see anything wrong with watching endless repeats of The Big Bang Theory. It helps me get through lonely evenings. Nothing else helps. I could have worse coping skills. It may not be the healthiest way to hang with "friends", but it works for me. If I feel a little less alone after watching a couple episodes, than I have coped well.

Another aspect of watching The Big Bang Theory that is important for me is that it helps me experience things I do not always encounter like laughter and companionship. When you are depressed, you do not laugh often. It is just difficult to experience things that are funny. But when my television friends engage in hijinks, I can laugh with them. I assume I have chosen a comedy for my go-to television show because I need to laugh. It makes sense. My world is often dark, and comedy provides a glimpse of the light.

When I watch The Big Bang Theory, I feel like I am a part of a group. I do not really have a social group. Most of my friendships are one on one. I do not know what it is like to have a circle of friends, to have a group of people who all care about each other. The characters on The Big Bang Theory fill that void. It is not the most solid way to fill that void, but it serves its purpose for me. Even though the experience is not real, when I watch television, I am a part of something.

In real life, those characters would not likely have someone like me around. The safety of a television allows me to pretend that it could happen. I could be accepted by others. I could have friends and live a life filled with happier times. In my reality, that does not happen.

The routine and repetition of watching the same television show comforts me in some way. It creates a world for me that does not exist in my real life. It works for me. Would I like to have real experiences like the show allows me to participate in? Definitely. But for now, I have to settle for a television show. Maybe my healing journey will eventually bring me to a point where I can engage in relationships that are real. I can hope, but I do not know when that will happen. So for now, I will watch The Big Bang Theory and enjoy the company of my fictional friends.

23

Final Thoughts

The Woman in the Mirror

As I gaze into the cracked mirror,
My inner soul is reflected.
I see the past unfold within the eyes looking back at me.
She alone knows all I have been through and all I will become.
Scars left by trials
Imprinted their marks upon my heart.
Yet a strength I didn't know I possessed emerges.
The cracks slowly disappear.
The woman in the mirror smiles.
At last, I know I am the woman in the mirror.

Depression and anxiety do not define me. These illnesses are my diagnosis, but they are not who I am. Their presence in my life definitely affects me. Weakened at times, I am still resolute in not allowing my illness to define who I am as a person. For years I have fought to overcome depression and anxiety. I have won some of the battles and lost others. No doubt that pattern will continue.

The myriad of medications I have tried proved ineffective in truly healing me. Yet I am blessed because I have a mental health team that understands me and works with me. They guide my healing; lift me up when I am struggling. Not one of them dictates how I will be treated. They regard me as a valuable member of my mental health team. I am no longer alone on this healing journey. Dr. Klein, Dr. Sullivan, and Stephanie Debnath support me. As I have tried to express throughout this book, I am eternally grateful to them.

I am at peace with my diagnosis. Depression and anxiety are a part of my life. No permanent escape exists. However, healing is possible if I accept healing as a journey, not a destination. Ups and downs will continue to exist. TMS will always be a part of my life. I have accepted this fact. I welcome it because I know it offers me times of wellness. TMS has given me the gift of hope. TMS is one of my teammates on this journey.

For so long I hid my mental illness or tried to hide it. I was ashamed of the depression and anxiety. Shame cost me. I lost experiences; missed out on many of life's offerings. I cannot get those back. There is no use in feeling sorry for myself. Those times are over. I must move forward. Shed the shame and live. Depression and anxiety impact my life, but they no longer control it.

I am working on regaining control over my life. Mental health advocacy is a major part of that effort. By advocating for mental health care, I am allowing my voice to be heard. Sharing my experiences assists others in finding their voices and traveling the healing journey. Together we can be a mighty force. Our histories are filled with pain, but hope awaits in our presents.

Every time I speak about mental health, I experience a piece of healing. Hope is reflected in the eyes of my audience. As I share my story, I ease some of my pain. I connect with others. Many can relate to my story. For some, the connection is personal suffering. Others connect through their care for a loved one who is suffering from mental illness. Still others provide professional care for those who suffer from mental illness. No matter what the connection, our stories resonate with each other. We share a common need for healing, a common desire to heal.

When I speak or write about mental illness, I am strengthened. Mental illness has stolen a lot from me, but it has also provided me with gifts. The gift of connection comes from those who hear my story and open up about their own stories. Our experiences may differ, but we find connection in the effects of mental illness. We relate in ways others cannot fathom.

When you are in the rabbit hole of depression, you want to know you are not alone. It is not that you want others to suffer. Rather you need to know it is not just you. I do not wish depression on anyone. It is painful to live with mental illness. It is also lonely. At times it feels as if no one else understands, as if the darkness surrounds only you. It is a horrible feeling. Depression and anxiety isolate individuals. The isolation can be devastating. You become numb to life and afraid to feel. Depression is painful and numbing at the same time. Opposite feelings existing simultaneously. Wishing to feel; not wanting to feel. It is difficult to explain how these two opposing feelings exist at the same time, but they do. It is part of the power of depression.

The power of depression and anxiety has ruled my life, but I have learned that I do not have to accept their control. I have the coping skills and the support to overcome their power. It will never be easy. Depression and anxiety will always be present to some degree. Illnesses like mine do not just go away, but I can choose to focus on the light. I can be positive about my ability to stand up and fight my illness. My experiences can help others. It took a long time and a lot of ups and downs, but I have chosen to use my experiences in a positive way.

This book tells my story. It is one of many stories lived by people with mental illness. We do not all have the means to share our stories. I do and I will tell my story to anyone who will listen or read. Stories like mine need to be shared. That is how we can attack the stigma that surrounds mental illness. Our stories will shatter the idea that we are victims who cannot fight back. Mental illness is a beast. It is a terrible illness, but it is one that can be battled. Those of us who suffer must join together and allow our voices to be heard.

One day mental illness will be treated like the health problem it is. It will not be stigmatized. It will be considered normal to see a therapist. There will be no shame in taking psychiatric medications. Mental health will be on equal ground with physical health. Employees will not have to be afraid to take a day off for their mental health. It will be accepted just the same as taking a day off because of the flu. Until that day, I will continue to advocate for mental health care.

Mental illness has taken me on a journey. It may not be the journey I wanted to undertake, but it is the journey I was handed. There has been a lot of darkness on my journey, but I have found light. My mental health team has brought me that healing light. Discovering TMS was a lifesaver. Learning that there can be times without depression and anxiety plaguing me has been amazing. I did not know I could live without that weight bearing down upon me. I urge others who suffer from mental illness to search for the treatment that works best for them. Do not be afraid to ask questions. Take risks. Treatment does not have to be a pill. Mental healthcare professionals are making great strides in treatment. We need to trust them, but at the same time use our own voice. Mental health care is a team effort. And we are a part of that team. We must remember that.

I have battled mental illness for over 35 years. I do not know a life without mental illness. What I have learned is that I can live despite my mental illness. It is my hope that this book shows that. In parting, my message is to take mental illness head-on and fight back.

My psychologist,
Dr. Richard Klein, and I.

My psychiatrist,
Dr. Catherine Sullivan, and I.

Psychiatric Nurse Practitioner at
TMS, Stephanie Debnath, and I.

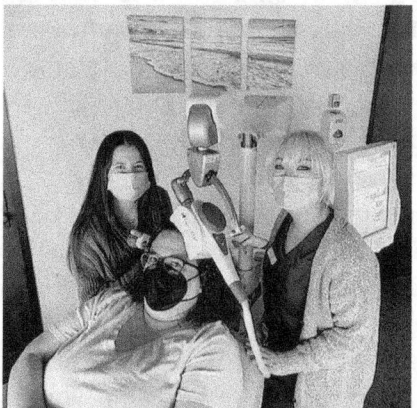

TMS nurse, Hanna and tech, Nidia,
and I during treatment.

Pam Martin, Carol Harrison, and I at my college graduation in 1996.

My friend, Carol Nichols, and I at one of my speaking events.

My friend, Sarah, and I after a night of painting, a bit of self-care.

My friend, Shannon Feldmann, and I celebrating the release of my third book.

My primary care provider, Cristina Rosales, and I.

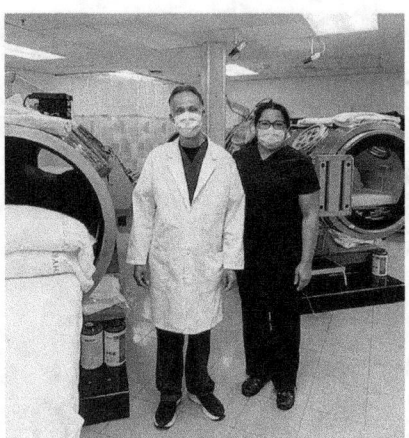

Hector and Lili next to the hyperbaric chamber.

My friend, Sharon Raaen, and I enjoying some music for self-care.

www.ingramcontent.com/pod-product-compliance
Lightning Source LLC
Chambersburg PA
CBHW082106140626
46553CB00018B/955